Security Analysis Essentials
Study Guide and Workbook
Volume 2

Created by: Pete Herzog
Marta Barceló Jordan
Bob Monroe

HACKING IS LEARNING
www.hackerhighschool.org

Table of Contents

 **WARNING**

Hacking is a methodology for learning and as with any learning tool there are dangers. Some lessons, if abused, may result in injury. Some additional dangers may also exist where there is not enough research on possible effects of emanations from particular technologies. Students using these lessons should be supervised yet encouraged to learn, try, and do. However the authors or ISECOM cannot accept responsibility for how any information herein is abused.

ISECOM

Introduction to the Security Analysis and Hacking Study Guide

There are hundreds of books written on networking and each one stands on its own merits. This book was not written to compete with any of those other works. This book was written to speed up the learning process and cut through some of the fluff. Don't bother to read our book if you want to know the names of people who wrote a certain protocol or dates when specific networking milestones occurred. If you want to know which university designed a certain networking function or which company patented a widget, than you picked up the wrong book.

We wrote this manual for speed of learning and ease of information retention.

We are not teaching you to be cracker, rather we are teaching you to work on contemporary and future systems. If you want to be a mechanic, you have to learn how to dissemble an engine. To be a successful network security professional, you need to know the inner workings of your digital world. This world includes portable devices (BYOD), servers, network protocols, hardware, software, security frameworks, principles of trust, virtual machines and dozens of other items.

Flipping through the pages you will notice that this book is not your typical technical guide. We designed everything to keep the reader engaged; to keep you interested. You will find segments like **Feed Your Head**, which are focused on deeper aspects of a topic. There are exercises that aren't just multiple choice questions but require you to actually think through a problem or research to find them. This is not a Dummies guide. This is a Hackers guide; old school hacker style.

The lessons from HackerHighschool.org which this manual follows and expands on have been an enormous task on behalf of the nonprofit Institute for Security and Open Methodologies (ISECOM.org).

Our guiding philosophy is to encourage all people across the world to embrace technology for its uses but not to harm others. Information should be free to the extent that it doesn't infringe on personal privacy or global peace.

So You Want to Do Security Analysis Like a Hacker?

The hardest part of hacking is the analysis. Most students learn the *skills* part of security testing pretty quickly, and a few of them are natural hackers, automatically showing the right combination of resourcefulness, tenacity, and creativity. However, it's extremely rare to find a natural at security analysis, and although good experience makes a better security analyst, it doesn't refine the skill.

There are things you will be confronted with when working in professional, real-world security that you won't find correct answers for in a checklist or a book. You also won't learn the answers through experience because analysis is always a unique experience. For most everyone, it only can come from learning proper security analysis skills. Human minds are designed to conform what we see with the notions of what we know. If we don't know it then we can't see it, at least not the way we need to see it for analysis. There's been many studies on this and whether it's part of change blindness or cognitive bias, we basically see what we've been told to see. So don't blame yourself if you find it hard to analyze security because it's not a normal trait in society.

Society is no more designed to assure that people have good analysis skills than it is designed to assure that we have good security skills. We know we don't because, otherwise, trust wouldn't be the centerpiece of human relationships and compromise wouldn't be the centerpiece of a community. The odd thing is that it's not human nature to be bad at analysis. We have the capacity. We can learn it. It's just that as a society it's not encouraged. So this is something you will have to overcome.

Of course, it's easy to invoke doom and gloom about the one obscure piece of knowledge dangling out of your reach. But it's not out of your reach. You have to choose not to learn it. You have to choose to ignore it. The problem is that most people think they do security analysis at least better than average and ignore the signs that they might not. If you want to be good at security analysis, and I hope you do, then take every opportunity to pick apart every security product to see what it really does, every vulnerability to see how it really works, every attack to see what really happened. Do this and it won't take long to figure out how much you don't know, the first step toward making a good security analysis.

Hacking Malware

Introduction to Hacking Malware

It's amazing how easily **malware** exploits systems. Dr. Fred Cohen wrote his PhD dissertation on the idea of a virus back in 1984. It was published in 1985. The university found the dissertation profound and initially ridiculous until Dr. Cohen demonstrated his idea. This was around the time of the Morris worm. As soon as the academics saw the potential of a virus, it scared the hell out of them.

The school was afraid his dissertation might give bad guys some bad ideas. So they yanked the published product later in 1985, but the idea had already been planted and demonstrated even before the Cohen report.

The evolution of these products has led them to be made into weapons, for instance **Stuxnet**. The smallest replicating virus was only 90 lines long (and came out of MIT's Core Wars).

Malware can teach security professionals about social engineering, software exploits, stealth and advancements in technology that show the skills of some serious programmers. Newer forms of malicious programs can be extremely sophisticated and require teams of well-funded programmers to create. Other pieces are simple exploits cooked up in someone's bedroom that sneak past security controls and wreak havoc.

Malware didn't originally earn any money or bring any tangible gain (other than occasional ransomware) for the person who wrote the program. This changed over the years as malware creators learned to take advantage of data theft, using credit card information to get access into the global banking systems with the Zeus virus. Since then, this category has thrived.

Lots of new types of malware attempt to take advantage of you through scams, spam, bot-nets and spying. And it has created a billion dollar a year antivirus industry. Hmm, suppose there's any connection here?

When you dissect a virus, you get to see the inner workings of truly marvelous programs. Polymorphic, what an awesome idea! That's intelligent design, in our book. Why don't we have polymorphic Intrusion Detection Systems? It's tough to understand why malware writers use these wonderful techniques that giant software makers don't. Just like a real virus, we can learn how users think and how this software exploits human behavior to survive (and thrive).

Most Malware (or **mal**icious soft**ware**) is a computer program, or part of a program, that has damaging or unwanted effects on your computer. When people think of malware they think of a **virus**, but the term malware is about much more than just viruses. Our fun online friends have created **worms** and **Trojans**, **rootkits**, **logic bombs**, **spyware** and **botnets**. Malware can be any of these, or it can package several of these together. It's difficult to label malware today as simply a virus, worm or even worm/trojan. And that is why the generic term malware is more appropriate for our discussion.

Are you ready to dive in?

The AV-TEST Institute registers over 180,000,000 malware programs beginning from 1984. They add an additional 20,000 new samples per day. Check it out for yourself at http://www.av-test.org/en/statistics/malware/.

The problem is that we don't know how they categorize malware. For instance, polymorphic malware could look like lots of different virii, or the same one, or not be detectable at all. And intrusion detection systems will see different things than antivirus programs. Take all of these numbers with a big grain of salt.

Viruses (Virii)

This is what most people think of when they think of malware. Computer **viruses** came from computer science studies of artificial life – known then as cellular automata – which gradually became more "life-like," with the ability to propagate (make more of themselves), infect more hosts, become persistent, even hunt and kill each other. They resembled naturally occurring viruses in their behavior and thus the name stuck.

Viruses or **virii** are self-replicating pieces of software that, similar to biological viruses, attach themselves to another program, or, in the case of macro viruses, to another file. The virus is only run when the program is run or the file is opened. That's what makes viruses different from worms. If the program or file isn't accessed in any way, then the virus won't run and won't copy itself further.

Variants of viruses can use different trigger mechanisms like a certain time and date or a keystroke combination. These are usually designed for certain events such as remembrance of uprisings, crimes, acts of war or when the virus author's girlfriend puts out a restraining order against them.

Some malware consists of standalone programs that can appear to be software updates or pictures from someone's visit to the beach. Adobe PDF files have been a frequent launch point for many virus outbreaks, as well as Java. There are lots of reports of pirated software designed to look legitimate but that actually contains malware. That is why you need to look at the software **checksum** before downloading. Yes, **MD5 hash** values can be forged too, but we just want you be to as careful as possible when you download your legal copy of whatever you're getting.

A well-designed virus will evade detection, execute its payload and spread to other machines without the victim ever knowing what has happened until it's too late or maybe never.

Noted authority Dr. Fred Cohen lists some additional nasty ways malware can foul up your system and data:

- randomizing protection settings
- readable files become unreadable
- unreadable files become readable
- writable files become unwritable
- unwritable files become writable
- executables are not
- non-executables are
- setUID (trust level) privileges are set for untrusted programs
- when introduced into a competitor's manufacturing line it can lower the quality of products when the system is controlling a production operation (yikes!)

These days, you'll find that most malware is used as a payload delivery tool. A virus could be used to locate sensitive data in a network, open and keep open a connection for an attack, establish a DDoS, sniff financial information, or disrupt services such as manufacturing and infrastructure. Sophisticated malware will usually have several defense mechanisms, hold multiple exploits, and be written to survive and spread for as long as possible.

The Polymorphic Virus

Once we figured out what a virus was (after 1988), they were easy enough to detect. They had a certain signature to identify them, either within themselves as a method to prevent re-infection, or simply they had a specific structure which it was possible to detect such as a payload. Then along came the **polymorphic** virus, "poly" meaning multiple and "morphic" meaning shape. This new breed of viruses changed themselves each time they replicated, rearranging their code, changing encryption and making themselves look totally different. This morphing created a huge problem for detection, as instantly there were no longer good signatures to detect viruses.

One of the easiest ways to make a virus change itself is by simple encryption. All the virus author has to do is use a random key generator to change the virus and make it unrecognizable every time the virus was copied. The idea made it difficult for **antivirus (AV)** vendors to locate a common code string for their signature-based AV software. The source string code was different every time because of the encryption.

The AV vendors decided to look at which parts of a polymorphic virus could not change, which would be the encryption/decryption portions of the malware. As you might expect, the virus writers thought of methods to alter their decryption functions and make those as random as the rest of the program. Rogue programmers added alternating dates, random clocks, different algorithms, operations and all sorts of techniques to make the entire polymorphic virus as undetectable as possible.

Virus creators turned to other methods of hiding malware like breaking the code into several segments. The first virus segment would be a harmless PDF but inside the PDF was a scripting call to perform a download of some more of the virus. The second portion of the virus is encrypted so malware detectors don't notice the install.

The creators think of ways to make a virus look anything but like a virus. Since antivirus programs look for files, events, behavior, or suspicious activities that might be a virus, the polymorphic authors decided to mimic functions of the operating system, peripherals and users.

In some cases, the virus replaces the real system files with their own variations. Sweet: every time you, say, open Notepad, the virus replicates.

The Macro Virus

The **macro viru**s makes use of the built-in ability of a number of programs to execute code. Programs such as Word and Excel have limited, but very powerful, versions of the Visual Basic programming language. This allows for the automation of repetitive tasks and the automatic configuration of specific settings. These macro languages can be exploited to attach viral code to documents, which will automatically copy itself on to other documents and propagate.

Since Word and Excel were built to operate as part of a suite of programs (Microsoft Office), a macro virus could take advantage of those special operating system privileges to spread its payload across entire corporate networks with ease. Office programs are allowed to use special (undocumented) developer calls and scripts within the operating system for increased productivity, which also gives macro viruses access to protected areas of the operating system and network.

In most email clients, you can preview an attachment without opening the email. This is where a macro virus will attack, since a mini program is opening the attachment. That preview will activate the attachment even if the file is labeled "cutepuppy.jpg." File labels can be spoofed.

You can expect to find macro-type malware wherever there are client-side executable scripts, code, forms or sub-routines. This often occurs with HTML5, Java, Javascript and other add-ons that are part of browsers.

Exercises

Research these questions:

6.1 What was the first virus? Don't trust the first answer you find. Check multiple sources. Five extra points for each classmate you can prove wrong.

6.2 Now: what was the first virus to be *released into the wild?* How did it propagate?

6.3 The **Klez** virus is well known for **spoofing**. What is spoofing, and how does Klez use it? Assume your computer is infected with Klez. How do you remove it? How do you find out?

6.4   Can a virus be useful or serve a useful function besides being evil? Think of the actual purpose of a virus before you make your decision.

6.5   What was the purpose of the Stuxnet virus? Based on what you read, did the virus achieve its goal(s)?

6.6   You just received an email with the following Subject: "Warning about your email account." The body of the message explains that your inappropriate use of email will result in your losing Internet privileges and that you should see the attachment for details. But you haven't done anything weird with email as far as you know. Are you suspicious? You should be. Research this information and determine what virus is attached to this message. (HINT: When you start thinking of breakfast – you're correct.)

Game On: The Malware Teacher

The technology classroom stank like old fish and maybe rat fur but was at least laid out in orderly rows. Each desk had a sleeping computer monitor resting on it. Fly-encrusted florescent lights flickered against the sunlight from the row of windows. One student in front yawned and the rest of the class caught it, spreading towards the back rows. The teacher, Mr. Tri, hunched over the screen on his desk, scowling.

If the room hadn't smelled so awful, people would have started eating their lunch, chewing gum or chatting while their teacher struggled with basic computer competence. But in the stench they pinched their noses or breathed through a sleeve. Talking, eating and chewing were the last thing anyone in the room wanted to do. Several already had eyes glued to the clock: fifty-two minutes to go.

Eight minutes late, Jace snuck in the room's backdoor as quietly as she could. The smell made her gag, a loud gag. Mr. Tri detected the sudden noise and the change in air pressure from the door opening. He spun around quick enough to see Jace before she could duck underneath a desk. "Jace. You decided to join us today. What a wonderful surprise."

The teen looked around the room and saw eyes telling her to run while she had the chance, make a break for freedom. Run, Jace, run. Save yourself!

She made eye contact with Mr. Tri and replied, "I apologize for my tardiness. I was sick in the bathroom." It was a lame excuse but the teacher was preoccupied with something even lamer. The hacker lowered her backpack and headed for her assigned desk. Pinching her nose, she asked one of her classmates what was going on. He replied, "You'll find out soon enough."

"Jace, since you missed this morning's introduction, I'll bring you up to date. Someone, one of you students, installed a flu or a cold on these computers," He said accusing everyone in the room."Now, until one of you fess up to the crime, you all will sit here enjoying this wonderful odor I brought in," Mr. Tri said. Jace looked around and saw the offending fur coat laced with sardines in the pockets, lying in the middle of the room.

"Ms. Jace do you know anything about this computer illness," he said as he pointed at the screen. Jace stood up and moved towards Mr. Tri as if she were approaching a hungry skunk. When she saw the text on the monitor and moved quickly to the keyboard and typed a few commands to see how the machine would respond.

"Hmm," she said to the screen. In a single motion, Jace reached into her backpack, pulled out her eyeglass case, opened it, and selected a USB thumb drive, thinking *gunslinger*. Her right hand was already typing while the left plugged in the drive. "Has anyone been updating the software on these computers?" The long silence had her imagining Mr. Tri's expression.

"What do you mean *update*?" he asked.

"Never mind."

First off, the browser was two versions old, and the Soda HTML extensions were famously exploitable by zero day vulnerabilities. Next, she saw another HTML5 product called Teepee that was two years old, at least. Clicking through folders of tools on the USB drive, Jace found and started Nmap to see what ports the computer was listening on. Nmap came back with a long list of open ports. Jace frowned.

Wireshark showed tons of TCP/IP traffic coming and going from five ports on the machine. To fix that, she simply unplugged the network connection. The five ports continued to send SYN packets, even without a network connection. She turned her attention to the operating system's start-up files.

Jace wasn't aware that she said "hmmm" all the time when she was examining a computer, but the rest of the class noticed it. They began to gather around her in a semi-circle of curiosity. "Hmmm," Jace said, spotting several unusual programs in the boot loading process and system start-up.

She scanned through each file directory looking for unusual folders and their files' last-access dates. Again, this brought up a list of highly suspicious programs, directories and files.

Every bit of the bad file stuff was under one user name account name. Jace slapped a hand over her mouth just in time, then slowly turned to her right, lowered her hand and said softly to him, "Mr. Tri, it looks like the one who downloaded all this malware is a user named Super Tri." It wasn't until the laughter started that she looked over her shoulder and saw the whole class gathered behind her.

Oops.

Game Over

Worms

Worms are similar to viruses in that they propagate, but they use network services to move around. But they don't rely on someone running or accessing a file to trigger the self-replicating code; it executes on its own as soon as it can find a vulnerable host.

So a worm is a standalone program that, after it has been started, replicates without any need for human intervention. It will move from host to host, taking advantage of an unprotected network or service. Worms have overloaded severs and entire networks because of they're all about multiplying. Depending on how the worm was designed, a worm may not have a specific end point or target.

Worms have been used to map networks, to dig into hidden areas and to report their findings at predetermined connection points. This type of malware can be autonomous or work within a command and control structure.

There are several instances of worms in major systems in which nobody has been able to remove them, determine their purpose or keep taps on their location. Worms are excellent for reconnaissance because they don't normally have a payload and use covert channels for communication if the communicate at all. If the worm never communicates, it's impossible to tell where it is and what it is supposed to do.

The good news for worms is that they usually only infect a system once. The bad news is about trying to locate that infection to remove the worm: Good luck.

Worm:Win32 Conficker

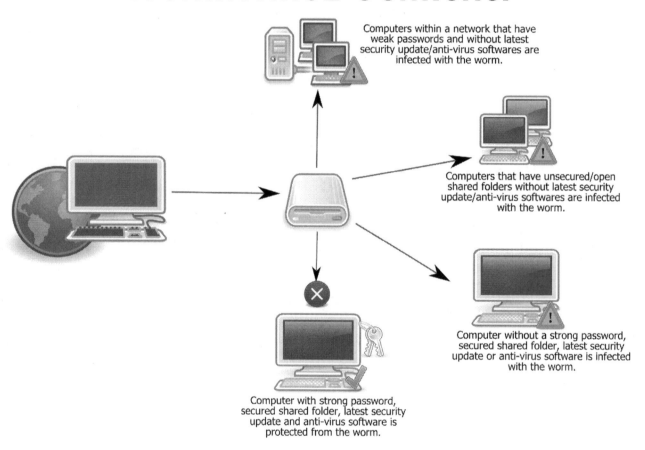

Figure 1. *How the **Conficker** Worm Spread. Photo courtesy of Wikipedia under Creative Commons. http://en.wikipedia.org/wiki/File:Conficker.svg*

Exercises

6.7   Which OSs were vulnerable to the first worm to spread over the Internet? Find the source code. Yes, really. No, it will not set your computer on fire. You can open the files in your browser and see how much fun the author was having. Curse him or envy him, depending.

6.8   Search for videos that show you how to use a worm hack tool. (Hint: use exactly that last phrase.) DO NOT CLICK ON THE LINKS. Considering that worms propagate through infected media like videos, why wouldn't you necessarily trust those videos? Or even those links?

6.9   How can you make a good decision to trust or not to trust these videos? For a start, do an Internet search and find the article, "Ten Tricks to Make Anyone Trust You (Temporarily)." Are any of these tricks being used on you?

Trojans and Spyware

The bread and butter of malware falls into the category of spam. This is **trojan** and **spyware** with a touch of **adware** for an extra kick. The original **Trojan Horse** was created by the Greeks several thousand years ago. (Think about the film "Troy" if you've seen it). The basic concept is that you offer something that appears useful or benign to sneak something nasty into an otherwise secure computer. Examples include: game trailers; e-mail promising naked pictures of your favorite celebrity; a program, tool or utility; a file, such as a PDF; or pirated videos. You will often find them loaded into so-called **freeware** games. The concept of freeware is not to fill a free product with advertising or junk, but somehow that idea got mixed up.

Trojans are pieces of malware which masquerade as something either useful or tasty in order to get you to run them. There are at least two types of trojans. The first breed of trojan malware pretends to be a useful program, picture, music, movie, or is an attachment within a program. The second type is a fake program that replaces the legitimate one on your system. Once they are inside a system they may do something unpleasant to your computer such as install a backdoor or rootkit, or – even worse – turn you machine into a zombie. Cue scary music in the background.

Your first clue that a trojan has been installed on your computer might be a massive slowdown and loss of resources. Your computer that is, not you. If you have a massive slowdown of your body and/or loss of resources then you have the flu. Go get a shot from your doc. Your computer is not so easy to fix. You are going to need your strength.

You might notice some applications won't load, or programs load that shouldn't be running at all. Don't expect your antivirus software to help because it didn't stop that trojan from installing; why should it work now?

Nope, this is all your mess and if you have one trojan on your computer, expect to find more. Since trojans are just vessels for dumping junk on your computer, you will need to figure out where the trojan came from. What was the last thing you downloaded, opened up or viewed from a friend?

To be fair to your friend, even very large organizations have given their employees, customers, and each other trojans before. Sony did it. Valve did it, twice. Microsoft may have done it but they keep calling them "undocumented features."

We are going to talk about destroying malware later.

Rootkits and Backdoors

Often when a computer has been compromised by an attacker, they'll want to get back into the machine. There are many variations on this, some of which have become quite famous – have a look on the Internet for **"Back Orifice."**

Rootkits and backdoors are pieces of malware that create methods to keep access to a machine or network. They could range from the simple (a program listening on a port) to the very complex (programs which will hide processes in memory, modify log files, and listen to a port). Both the Sobig and MyDoom viruses install backdoors as part of their payload.

Both hardware and software manufactures have been accused of installing backdoors in products. Some of this is state-sponsored hacking, while some is just nosy companies. Sony installed spyware on users devices to enforce **Digital Rights Management (DRM)**. China has been charged with installing secret code in routers, hubs, and other products built in their country. These tactics have destroyed consumer trust in brands and products made in certain countries.

When you are dealing with rootkits, expect to lose your **master boot record (MBR)**, the *software* that boots your OS. Rootkits need to load themselves into memory before the operating system. They do this by hiding portions of themselves in the MBR. This means that successful removal of the rootkit will also damage your MBR.

To fix the MBR you will need to get to the command prompt through system recovery. At the command prompt, enter the following command and then hit enter:

bootrec.exe /FixMbr

If successful, you should be greeted with the message "**The operation completed successfully.** The Master Boot Record has been repaired."

While the above command does fix the MBR, there still might be an error with the system partition's **boot sector** and **Boot Configuration Data (BCD)**, which is to say there might be a *physical* issue to fix. This can happen if you install another operating system alongside Windows 7, such as Windows XP. To write a new boot sector, try the following command:

```
bootrec.exe /FixBoot
```

Exercises

6.10   Research Back Orifice. What exactly does it do? Who created it?

6.11   Research Windows Remote Desktop. What exactly does it do? Compare it to Back Orifice: how are they different?

6.12   Let's say you have a computer you want to make your computer dual-bootable, able to start two different versions of Windows. There's a trick to it, though (as usual). In what order must you install the Windows versions for this to work?

Logic Bombs and Time Bombs

Logic bombs and time bombs are malware programs that sit quietly until some condition is met – perhaps a particular bit of data or a certain date. They do not normally propagate.

For example: a program could be created that, should the administrator fail to log in for more than three weeks, would start to delete random bits of data from disks.

This occurred in a well-known case involving a programmer at a company called General Dynamics in 1992. He created a logic bomb that would delete critical data, set to be activated after he was gone. He expected that the company would then pay him significant amounts to come back and fix the problem. However, another programmer found the logic bomb before it went off, and the malicious programmer was convicted of the crime and fined $5,000 US dollars. The judge was merciful – the charges the man faced in court carried fines of up to $500,000 US dollars, plus jail time.

In 2009, a terminated employee at the mortgage loan giant Fannie May placed a logic bomb that was set to wipe out their 4,000 servers. Luckily, the malware was spotted before it activated. It wasn't such a lucky break for the ex-employee, though.

A logic bomb/time bomb is usually an insider attack committed by a disgruntled employee, contractor, or fired employee with access to the network. Prevention is the best method to stop this kind of threat. Enforce separation of duty so that no person has too much power over a system. Make sure every employee takes a vacation each year so that an evil doer can't keep covering their tracks.

And best of all, if your company fires somebody, take way their network access immediately. Don't let the employee finish up the day or check a few emails. Get them out of the office building, right after you take away their building access keys (codes). Place their network account in a special folder but remove all privileges for user access, especially remote access. That ought to help out some (as long as they don't know other employee's passwords).

Exercises

6.13   What reasonable (and legal) uses might there be for time bomb and logic bomb coding?

6.14   How can you detect such a program on your system?

Game On: Cookies and Code

As boring as her time in the apartment was, Jace always enjoyed the comfort of her small room. After climbing three flights of stairs, she touched the dirty rail along the third floor. The rail was burning hot in the sun thanks to the black paint job, with years and years worth of coating underneath. Her hand jumped away.

The next door was where Sweet G and Jace lived. Nothing fancy, nothing glamorous, and certainly nothing to brag about, but it was home and therefore it was sanctuary.

As Jace reached for the screen door, a voice was coming from inside the room. *Maybe G's got company*, she told herself. Jace didn't want to disturb her grandmother since she rarely got visitors. With utmost caution, the grandchild snuck through the doorway, making sure she didn't allow the squeaky screen door to alert G or her guest. *Be the wall* she told herself as she attempted to move silently along the front hall towards her own bedroom.

"Registry start-up has a 'look-up' call to a hidden directory in privileged area of certain..." Jace heard coming from down the other hallway leading to grandma's bedroom. *What the heck?* Jace had never heard this type of talk coming from Sweet G. *There must be someone with her.*

The teen stopped trying to be so quiet and walked towards her grandmother's bedroom to find out what the conversation was all about. The room smelled like old books and denture cream. Again, Jace heard Sweet G talking to someone. "Alright, two can play this little game," G said from her room.

Jace pretended like she hadn't heard anything, "Hi Sweet G, how was your day?" There was no one else in the room but her grandmother, who was quick to turn off the monitor when Jace entered the room.

"Oh hi dear, how was school? Did you do anything interesting today? How much..." G tried her best to change the odd behavior of getting caught in the act of doing something she wasn't supposed to be doing.

There were four books spread open on the quilted bed cover. Jace had never seen these books and now the suspicious behavior got Jace really interested. Jace causally moved into G's bedroom, looking around for the smoking gun. Without an invitation, she sat on the end of the bed near G's computer and the open books.

"Grandma, would you like to explain to me what you are doing," Jace squinted detective eyes.

G looked around for the best answer she could find, "Well darling, when you get to be my age you sometimes talk to yourself. It happ...."

Jace interrupted, "Oh, that's fine. I understand but I'm not concerned about you talking to yourself. I *am* concerned about what you were saying. You said words like registry, look-up calls and redirects."

Caught in the act, G wasn't going to give up her secrets so easily. G said, "I made some fresh lemonade. Why don't you get yourself a tall glass and grab some ginger cookies too." Grandma waved her hand: *Go on, leave me alone*.

But her inquisitive housemate wasn't going to give up so easily. "G, I know what I heard. You were talking to your computer as if you knew all about programming. How do you know about that stuff?" Jace folded her arms and pursed her lips.

"Well, honey. I don't have a clue about protacking a computer thing-a-ma-gig. I was just angry because some fool messed up my email," G said like a bad actor practicing her lines.

"Okay, then please explain these books you have on your bed," Jace countered. "*TCP/IP Network Administration* by Craig Hunt, hmm, or how about this one, *IPv6 Security*, or this other one," Jace was cut off by her grandmother.

"Now see here young lady. Those books belonged to your grandfather. I just opened them up to see if I could find a simple answer to this email cold I have. And those books are none of your business," G protested with an accusing finger pointing at her granddaughter.

Jace stood up from the bed. "But why your name is written on the edges of all of them?" Checkmate, G.

"Jace, how do you know that is my name."

Puzzled by the question, Jace replied, "Well it must be your name. It is printed right here on each, hmmm … It's gotta be your name."

"Dear, what you see along the book's edges is an initial and our last name. That initial is not mine, it belonged to your grandfather. Just because I can read a book doesn't mean I know what I'm doing. Now go along and bring us both a glass of lemonade."

Grandma had settled that argument rather nicely.

Jace frowned at the defeat. She hated to lose an argument. As the teen headed to the hallway, G stopped her one last time. "Darling, please add a few ice cubes to my glass."

With two plastic glasses in each hand and a cookie stuffed in her mouth, Jace returned to grandma's room. "Oh thank you sweety, I was getting thirsty fighting off all those accusations," G said with a sideways grin.

"So, what is the deal with your email," Jace wanted to change the subject to something other than her grandmother's overwhelming evidence of foul play.

Sweet G answered by clearing her throat, "Oh, I get these messages about trying to relay something, I don't know what it is."

"Oh, that's an easy fix, G. You didn't need to dig out all those books to fix something as simple as this. Here, let me see your keyboard for a minute," the teen wizard replied.

"Grandma, why do you have all these emails from the lottery? Nobody ever wins those things. Do these emails have anything to do with the random number asked Sweet G. "You are, aren't you!? You little devil you," she said, giving Sweet G a high five.

Game Over

Malware Today

Malware usually gives the attacker access to files or data on your computer, network, tablet or smartphone. Yes, your mobile phone can get malware too. **No computer system is immune from malware – including all personal electronics.**

Your mobile phone, or smartphone, is just a physically small computer. If you are surfing the web, using Facebook or opening email attachments, then you are vulnerable to malware on your phone. Malware may even come preinstalled. The issues are the same as with your computer; for example, you risk having your passwords hacked. More likely, the malware will wait for you to do some online banking and either clean out your bank account or steal your banking credentials and send them to the attacker.

Internet TV is also here. Now you can watch television and surf the Internet all at the same time. You can connect things up and have a "smart" home. Again, you'll have the same issues as you have on your computer. Researchers have hacked into Internet enabled TVs, onboard computers on cars and even refrigerators. Pretty much anything with an onboard computer can be attacked. Be aware that criminals can infiltrate your home, a private space where you feel secure, through your online interactions.

You may think you have nothing of value on your computer or smartphone, but your identity can be exploited. That is, an attacker could take information about you from your computer or phone together with publicly available information about you, say your Facebook photo, and there may be enough information to build a detailed profile. The attacker could try and open credit cards, or take out bank loans, in your name. This is known as **identity theft**. Creditors will then expect you to pay them back for the things the *attacker* bought. It can take years to prove you didn't spend the money and to clear your good name. It could delay you getting a loan to buy that "fast and furious" car you've been dreaming of.

We are digitally connected almost 24 hours a day and we expect our devices to remain part of the Internet even when we are not using them. Malware creators like that. Our phones are synched to our tablets which are synched to our computers which are synched to our cloud accounts. All of this information is at our finger tips and we want access to our music, files, movies, and personal data everywhere we go. Malware creators like that, too.

Currently, a lot of malware targets mobile devices. These devices have the least amount of security yet have the same accessibility to your data as a computer. On your computer, you probably have a firewall, antivirus software, and anti-spyware software installed. Your mobile devices probably don't have any of these protective measures. That needs to change.

Malware creators may be changing tactics away from ransom and denial of service attacks towards complete destruction of an organization's network data. Sony was attacked in October 2014 in a multipronged effort to release incriminating evidence, while destroying vital data in the background. This cyber assault used sophisticated malware against Sony to disrupt daily operations and render critical data useless.

Feed Your Head: Threat Flavors

According to a joint research project between ISECOM and Barkly called the Open Source Cybersecurity Playbook (isecom.org/playbook), malware is used in the majority of modern threats.

1. Phishing
2. Social Engineering
3. Ransomware
4. Drive-by Downloads
5. Download Hijacking
6. Malvertising
7. Zero-Day Attack
8. Password Cracking
9. Distributed Denial of Service Attackers
10. Scareware
11. SQL Injection

Exercises

6.15 Know the latest malware threats. That is, what new malware threats have emerged today? Go to the website of an antivirus software company and search for their threat monitor. Do an Internet search on "threat research and response."

6.16 Are there any threats that affect social networking sites? Look at different antivirus websites. Do they agree on what the latest threat is? How often do malware threats change (how many new ones are released each day)? How often should you update your anti-malware?

6.17 What are the issues relating to malware that could arise when you bring your own device (BYOD), say a laptop or smartphone, and connect it to a network at a friend's house, or at your work? What about coffee houses or restaurants?

Attackers have various motivations, but for the modern malware writer it is usually financial gain: to rob people of their money. They don't have to break into your house any more. They may empty your bank account, or spend big in your name. The other way that malware makes money is using your computer to distribute spam or phishing emails. Attackers can make a lot of money this way. That is, until your ISP blocks you.

In an even more ironic turn, crackers have come out in the open, offering malware as a service. An easy search will find you a botnet for rent or a cracker for hire to write custom malware. Could you trust a malware writer? Can they leave themselves some sort of backdoor into *your* computer?

Mobile Malware

Attackers used to focus on the network, but now they can easily circumvent the network defenses by targeting business mobile devices instead. In these next exercises, we will look at building malware for Android tablets and phones. Since almost all of these devices connect to a network in one way or another, there is a pretty good chance that they will log onto the company network at some point. Of course, many of the networks offer remote access but only for isolated segments of that network. This isn't true for web based services though and has become a weak spot for many companies' security.

Android runs as a virtual machine (VM) with a rebranded Linux flavor, designed for small devices but built for speed. The VM is called "Dalvik" in case you were wondering, which is a Java VM with much less overhead (demand for resources). The OS is built in C++ as are all the libraries included in the Android Software Development Kit (SDK). This means that there is a Linux kernel underneath all that GUI fluff. What this also means is that Android can run Java applications inside browsers and as standalone programs.

Third party programs can run native APIs to access built-in functions of Android like the Resource Manager, Telephone Manager and other main controls. This is a major vulnerability since there aren't many reasons for a game to have access to your location, photos, text messages or other private data. The third party applications are often written in Java while system applications are written in C++ (complied for the processor in use).

Exercises

6.18 Explore your own device's Android APKs (applications). Head over to http://developer.sonymobile.com/knowledge-base/tools/ and look for APKAnalyser. This free tool will show you how that APK works and which APIs are called. It will also show you a very nice graphic of how that app works as a flowchart.

6.19   What are some of the ways we can determine where the device owner is?

6.20   Head over to http://www.xray.io/#vulnerabilities and take at look at known vulnerabilities for Android operating on an Arm processor. If you were writing malware, which of the listed issues would you try first? Remember that they are listed in alphabetical order, not by popularity. Most phones run on an Arm core.

An Apple a Day

Now it's Apple's turn to be inspected. Apple has always marketed itself as being safe from malware because of the closed operating system and advanced security features. In truth, security in iOS for all Apple mobile devices depends on users only obtaining software from the official Apple Store. For jailbroken devices, this security feature can be bypassed, which means the Apple Store isn't an effective method to protect those devices. If the company relied solely on the protection offered by users purchasing software through official channels, than it isn't much of a practical plan at all.

Users like to share photos, attachments, messages, links and all kinds of other data. The shared data becomes an entry point for malware infections, just as with any operating system. Part of the reason we haven't seen much malware for iOS is because it is a relatively new popular platform. As iPhones and iPads become more attractive, they also become a larger target for malicious hackers. Now Apple products are a large player in the mobile community so they are getting much more attention from malware writers.

One of the first prime-time malicious programs for the iPhone is called **Wirelurker**. This application spreads using the enterprise provisioning system, which is a function that allows a company to install custom applications without having to go through Apple Store approval. Luckily the malware doesn't do much beyond loading up a comic book unless the phone is jailbroken. Those phones will have payment information slurped up and sent back to a command and control server. Other proof of concept programs have been demonstrated in the past and shrugged off by Apple as "impossible." Yet the whole idea behind a proof of concept is to show that it is possible.

Anything that connects to the Internet is susceptible to getting hacked by way of malicious links, click-jacking, redirects, Java exploits plus a ton of other vulnerabilities. Apple products are no different.

Exercises

6.21 Wirelurker is thought to compromise up to 800 million Apple users by using desktop to USB infection of iPhone and iPads. Why do you think such a powerful program uses a simple payload of installing a comic book application when it could install more dangerous software?

6.22 Look up exploit CVE-2014-4377 to see which operating systems and/or devices may be impacted. How would this exploit work if the user doesn't have Internet access? Safari will open up a rogue PDF even without Internet connectivity. Because this is an issue with the way Safari tags PDFs as images, multiple PDFs could be loaded up without the users knowledge, thus causing a buffer overflow that could be exploited.

6.23 The web page http://www.exploit-db.com/platform/?p=ios lists a collection of known vulnerabilities in iOS, which affect iPhone and iPad devices. Many of the items listed in the database involve multiple vulnerabilities ranging from Wi-Fi access to camera control. The database for iOS vulnerabilities only goes back to 2010. Which year has the largest collection of documented exploits and what do you think is the reason?

Botnets

A **botnet** is usually several hundred up to millions of computers that have been attacked, compromised, and have a **rootkit** and **backdoor** installed without the owners' knowledge. They are unwitting hosts to malware, or **zombies**. The attacker (**bot master** or **bot herder**) can remotely command those machines to do anything he wants, from sending spam, to DDoS attacks, to stealing financial information.

If your computer is infected with a bot, it could be used in an attack. An infected computer could be responsible for an attack on the police servers. Legally, you are responsible for the behavior of your computer, just like you are for your cat or dog. What if your computer was involved in an attack on critical infrastructure in your country, like power or water supply plants?

Those kinds of attacks are called **cyberwar**, though that's a dangerous word, because what the police do is very different from what armies do.

Who is behind botnets? Sometimes individuals, but usually organized crime gangs. You certainly don't want to mess with that lot! It is said that the next war (on Earth, not in the galaxy) will be fought in cyberspace.

Would you like to be a botnet hunter? There are a few dedicated individuals who do this. The problem is that, in order to hunt down and bring down a botnet, it's possible that you'll break some laws in the process. We'd best leave this to the professionals. They need to conduct their investigations within the constraints of the law.

Botnets are also used for **denial of service** attacks (**DoS**). Some of the recent DoS attacks have demanded money in exchange for calling off the attack. In the past, most DoS attacks relied on overwhelming servers with data requests in order to shut the servers down or force a reboot of the system. Some bot-nets have owned tens of thousands of machines which direct a single attack against another network to disrupt communication and thus business.

The bot-nets are individual computers located throughout the world but are controlled by one or more **command and control** (**C&C**) servers. Each machine is controlled by the C&C servers and told what and where to attack. The C&C servers are themselves controlled by another server called the mothership. By having layers of separate communications between the hackers and the attacking machines, locating the criminals behind the attacks is difficult.

Free Stuff

People want their favorite music, TV shows, movies and more for free. Think again! How do you think an attacker might spread their malware? An effective way to spread malware (and build a botnet) would be to attach it to something that everyone wants for free. So be careful what you install.

Delivery Techniques

Very few people would purposely put malicious software on their own system so malware creators need a way to install their products without a user's knowledge. There are several techniques that have proven themselves effective ways to install programs without the owners knowing it. Some of the best methods are repackaging, updates, and attachments (SMS, email, web links, and other malicious URLs).

Repackaging involves the use of real programs that are offered as legitimate software through distribution systems. Malware builders would take that software and add their malware to it or recompile the code to include their payload. Google Play has had a difficult time controlling legitimate programs for Android devices. Since most users don't pay attention to the original size of the correct program, it is fairly simple to replace a good copy with a malicious copy.

Software updates are another area where malware creators can fool users into installing their programs. The malicious programmer is able to persuade a user into downloading an update for some software on the user's computer. The update advisory looks legitimate and may even point the initial URL to an actual software patch. The URL or update link is actually loading up malware while telling the user that their program is being updated. This technique has been done with Adobe, Microsoft, Java, and several other well known vendors.

We've already discussed attachments as a method for distributing malware. Yet, web links are still the easiest way for malicious software to appear of a system. Browser plug-ins for running Javascript, Ajax, PDF openers, PHP, Flash and other programs allow malware to sneak in from malicious web pages. This means that you have to be on the look out for every possible access point when you are behind your keyboard.

One of the more interesting methods of installing malware is the use of multi-stage insertion. The malicious code is moved onto a user's system in sections to avoid detection. For example, a user might come across a link on a web site or a corrupt execution call inside the web browser from that web address. That single event allows a small program to run in the background of the machine. The program would make a minor adjustment to the system that opens a port or bypasses some security feature. Once that step is complete, another program is loaded that might just be the payload or could be a second-stage attack.

This process of multiple stage program loading can go on for as long as it is needed in order to install the malware and carry out an attack. Usually multi-stage malware is sophisticated enough that it is gathering information from large data sets, such as financial institutions or credit card database information. The massive attack on the American merchandise firm Target in late 2013 used a multi-stage attack that was updated at least five different times during the course of the breach.

Besides your typical file delivery mechanisms, some malware programmers are using communication channels built into computers to propagate. One particular program called **Flame** could use the system's own Bluetooth radio to transmit the malware to other machines nearby. Wi-Fi is also being used to transmit malicious code across airwaves. There has been rumors about some malware using high frequency audio tones to send bits to other devices. This technique has been proven to work in laboratory settings with super quiet environments. Don't expect this to work very well around your house though. You talk too loud and snore.

Countermeasures

There are a number of ways that you can detect, remove and prevent malware. Some of these are common sense, others are technical alternatives. This section provides a brief explanation and examples.

Antivirus Software

Antivirus software is available in many commercial and open source versions. These all use similar methods. They each have a database of known viruses, and they match the signatures of these against the files on the system to see if there are any infections (this is often called the **blacklist** approach). Often though, with modern viruses, these signatures are very small, and there may be false positives, things that appear to be viruses but are not.

Some virus scanners employ a technique known as **heuristics**, which means that they have a concept of how a virus behaves and try to determine if an unknown application matches these criteria. More recently, antivirus software has also crossed the boundary into **Host-based Intrusion Detection**, by keeping a list of files and checksums in order to increase the speed of scanning.

And yes, Apple Macs get malware too. Current estimates show 5,000 different types of malware for Apple products. There are exploit kits specifically designed to attack Macs. There are now numerous antivirus software programs for Macs. Search online for antivirus for Mac.

Do you use an antivirus on your iPhone or iPad? On your Android phone or tablet? On your Internet-connected TV or disc player? On your Linux box? Why don't you? Is antivirus software mandatory?

> There's a list of free software and processes to fix malware problems located at https://www.soldierx.com/tutorials/Malware-Removal-Guide.

Removing Unwanted Guests

Some malware is easier to remove than others. If you come in contact with some nasty virus, trojans or ransomware most antivirus software can remove the threat in a few seconds. There are other types of malware that don't go away very easy and require some research and work to remove, like rootkits. Some types of malware are almost impossible to remove without doing some damage to the data on that system.

One of the first steps to remove unwanted software to to figure out what it is: you need to identify the malicious software. Most antivirus software scans will provide you with a name and it's up to you to research that type of software. The key is to have several different antivirus scanners on hand because one is never enough. Once you know the name of the malware, head over to http://www.malwareremovalguides.info and see what they recommend for removing that threat.

Each type of malware may need to be treated differently so do your research before you start deleting files off of a machine.

More times than not, if you have one virus you will also have several more hiding elsewhere. It's not uncommon to locate several dozen different strains of trojans sitting alongside adware or rootkits. Deal with each, working on the worst infections first.

Malware Analysis

Imagine you work for an antivirus company and you discover new malware code that has never been detected before. You will need to assess the damage it could cause and what its intentions are, document and catalog the new malware, and most importantly, name it after yourself. Imagine that!

It would be a really bad idea to run malware on your own computer, or a shared computer connected to a network, for obvious reasons. If malware analysis seriously interests you, there is a lot more you need to know and you are going to need a test system exclusively for this purpose. It is pretty easy to write your own simple malware code or search online for virus code. Please be careful when you're getting into the "dark side" of the Internet. Malware writers are actual people, often with malicious and criminal intent; you don't want to hang out with them or invite them into your home.

With static analysis, it is possible to study a program without actually executing it. Tools of the trade are **disassemblers**, **decompilers**, and **source code analyzers.** Program disassembly involves converting a program file into a listing of machine language instructions; program decompilation is converting machine language instructions into the equivalent higher-level language source code; and static analysis is examining a program without actually executing it.

What if the malware is encrypted? If the code is encrypted, your job just got a bit harder but not impossible. Malicious code that is encrypted is usually a sign that the program is a multi-stage application. The stage of code that decrypts the program could already be somewhere else on the computer. You will need to look around for any script or application that downloaded around the same time that the malware was delivered.

For regular malware the usual procedure is to install and run it in a virtual machine. Depending on the type of malware, whether it is a stand alone executable, a Java app, a script or something else, you will need to decompile the program inside a sandbox on the virtual machine. This is not for the faint of heart. Most malware has already been decompiled and cataloged by other researchers. You can save yourself time and effort by looking up this information and following it like a roadmap.

Two sites for loading up malware are virusscan.jotti.org or www.virustotal.com. These sites run the code past well-known antivirus software and tell you the results. There are several items that you will want to pay close attention to. They are:

- **Propagation:** How the malware spreads
- **Infection**: How it installs, and remains installed despite disinfection attempts
- **Self-Defense**: How it conceals its presence and resists analysis
- **Capabilities**: Software functionality available to malware owner

Hint: Never trust or click on a pop up screen offering you free antivirus software if it says your computer is infected. This is almost always malware!

Keep in mind that the file extension JAR is a compressed Java file. If you ever want to inspect a Java element, take a look at http://en.wikipedia.org/wiki/Decompiler or the JAD project at http://varaneckas.com/jad/.

Exercises

6.24 Go online and find a Sandobx application for your operating system. How does it work? What applications would you use it with?

6.25 Do you use a free antivirus software? No problem, but let's check it out. Go to the vendor's website and search for a comparison of the free software versus the commercial version (it's highly likely there is one). What's the difference between the two? What would you get for your money if you bought the full version?

6.26 Search in your favorite search engine for "compare antivirus software." Choose a current review (from this year). Which antivirus product is rated number one? What makes them different?

6.27 Now test your antivirus software to see if it has detected all the threats on your computer. First, go to a free online malware detector. Warning- if you have private or important data on this computer, don't run anyone's online anything. Only do this if it's your test computer system or if this is a brand you know and can trust. Then run the online scan. This may take some time so use your time wisely while you wait. Did it detect any malware your antivirus software missed? If so, why didn't your antivirus detect it?

6.28 Test your AV software using a fake virus file. Go to http://www.eicar.org/anti_virus_test_file.htm and read the "Antivirus or Anti-malware test file" information carefully. The file you will be testing is not an actual virus but rather designed to look like a virus to your antivirus software. Download the file. Wait to see what happens. What does your antivirus software do? Close your antivirus message, if you get one, and complete the download procedure.

6.29 Now click eicar_com.zip. This compressed zip file contains a fake virus. What happened when you attempted to open the file? Is your antivirus program detecting this file as malicious?

6.30 Using the Internet, find an example of a trojan and of spyware. See eicar.com again.

6.31 Search the Internet for examples of rootkits and backdoors.

6.32 Now consider: could you sandbox your web browser so that anything it downloads is also trapped in the sandbox? Is this an effective alternative to antivirus?

Game On: Pet Store Hacking

Phone calls like this one reminded Jace of the wretched smell of bird poop, hamster pee, fish algae and animal food, eaten or not. "Hey Jace, I need some help from ya. Swing by here and I'll treat you to a dinner, you know, family style," Mokoa offered.

"What do you need that's so important at this time of the afternoon?" she responded.

With birds squawking in the background and someone banging away on a keyboard next to him, Mokoa just said,"I'll show you when you get here. Oh, bring your eyeglass case, too." Mokoa rarely asked for help and when he did need help, it was usually for someone else.

Jace put away her phone and grabbed her essential red case in one single move, stowing everything in her satchel. The human eye is not trained well enough to see this sort of quick action unless it was slowed way down, like the way magicians show how they pull off card tricks.

Grandma heard a faint, "gotta go, won't be home for dinner," as she felt the brush of air pass through the apartment room. "Busy girl," Sweet G thought as she went back to fixing another night's dinner alone. "It's good that she's busy, it keeps her mind off of other things like cleaning up her room or talking with me," G pouted slightly.

The pet store was almost empty, not counting the jungle noises and farm manure odors. The glass front door was decorated with sun bleached advertisements for products they no longer sold. Jace pushed open the left door with the "Pull" sign on it. She didn't care, the doors opened either way. To make the most noise possible, you had to open the left door since it had a bell attached and a small magnetic alarm above. The parrots hated to magnetic alarm (ding-dong) and the hamsters went crazy whenever they heard the bell. It was Jace's grand entrance into her second home, the pet store where Mokoa worked.

"S'up," Jace leaped over the old wooden counter holding the cash register. Instead of landing like a rock star, she tripped over a cord and almost fell against Mokoa's rear end when she landed on her elbows.

"Look Jace, I know you want to suck up to me but you don't have to kiss my tush." Mokoa barely glanced over his shoulder to see her on the ground. His focus was on an old laptop, the kind of laptop that was missing keys but had plenty of dents. Jace knew that laptop; it sounded like someone had thrown a handful of marbles into a ceiling fan. The smoke wasn't a big deal, but the sparks tended to worry her during start-up.

Mokoa finally turned around to face his hacker friend, "My super deluxe mainframe here is slowing down. I can't even get onto the Internet without the connection timing out. When I check to see what services are running, I don't see anything out of the ordinary but my Wi-Fi light is flashing like crazy. It's like the thing is busy updating or something that's sucking up all the juice."

Jace replied, "Have you tried to hit it with a hammer? Hammers work great for me. Oh, wait, your super deluxe has been hit too many times by the floor. Gravity sucks dude."

"Naw, come on, give me some help. I got two reports due later this week and they're both on this computer. I need those reports or else I'll have to steal yours." The dude sounded stressed.

Jace cracked her knuckles and dug out her red eyeglass case from the satchel. "Step aside, my friend, this might get ugly. I need room to work so stand back and watch an expert do her thang" Jace teased.

Since the old computer was already running, sort of, Jace turned off the network connection and disabled the internal Wi-Fi card. The machine grumbled.

Next, Jace opened a command line window and typed ipconfig /all.

The black window lit up with a list of current TCP/IP connections, settings, DHCP and DNS. Although Jace had manually turned off the network connection and knocked the Wi-Fi card offline, one connection was persistently attempting to reestablish itself. The modem came back online and the network regained its valuable link back to that IP address.

"What was that! Did you just do that or did the computer do that on its own?" Mokoa said referring to the renewed connection.

"Nope, I did NOT do that. Whatever is eating up your resources just did that. It's calling home, like a command and control server somewhere," Jace stopped being serious and starting sticking out her tongue as a little child would. "You are a Zombie, Mokoa is a Zombie, nah, nah, nah. This is hilarious, you don't own this computer, somebody else does," she taunted. "Brains, must have brains, give me brains" she put out her arms straight and moved towards the bewildered teen like a zombie.

"Okay, funny girl. Where's my chainsaw," they both laughed at Mokoa's response. Mokoa wasn't into old horror movies like Jace was. He preferred action flicks.

The ex-zombie moved back to the clunky old laptop and pointed to the screen for her friend to see what was really going on inside his computer.

"See, right here your computer is doing everything it can to set up another connection to the command and control server, the one that's running your machine. When I disable the net connections, a program is trying to get that connection back. Dude, somebody pwned you. Since this program is able to access admin privileges and take over your precious super computer here, I'm here to tell you that you are officially part of a large network," Jace didn't bother to turn around to see if Mokoa was even there.

"Let's look at the evidence. You haven't updated your OS in years, your firewall doesn't exist, and you're not running any malware protection. To make matters worse, you are operating at admin level instead of being a regular user. I'd say that you got what you deserve," she snickered.

"Now, what? Can you fix it? I need this thing," Mokoa said, voice as desperate as she'd ever heard.

Jace rested against the wood counter with the sun to her back. Looking at the screen, shaking her head, looking back at Mokoa, shaking her head some more. "Depends," she replied.

With hands in the air like a person might surrender, he asked, "Depends on what?"

Jace replied, "What's for dinner."

Game Over

NIDS/NIPS

Network intrusion detection systems (NIDS) is similar to antivirus software. It looks for a particular signature or behavior from a worm or virus. It can then either alert the user (as an **IDS**, or **Intrusion Detection System**), or automatically stop the network traffic carrying the malware (as an **IPS**, or **Intrusion Prevention System**).

HIDS/HIPS

Host-based Intrusion Detection systems (HIDS), such as **Tripwire**, are capable of detecting changes made to files. It is reasonable to expect that an application, once it is installed, shouldn't change unless it's updated, so watching file information, such as its size, last modification date and checksum, makes it instantly obvious when something is wrong.

Firewalls

Worms propagate across the network by exploiting vulnerabilities on each host. Apart from ensuring that vulnerable services aren't running, the next best thing is to ensure that your firewall doesn't allow connections. Many modern firewalls will provide some form of packet filtering similar to a HIPS, and will drop packets matching a certain signature.

Sandboxes

The concept of a sandbox is simple. Your application has its own little world to play in and can't do anything to the rest of your computer. This is implemented as standard in the Java programming language, and can also be implemented through other utilities such as **chroot** in Linux. This restricts the damage that any malware can do to the host operating system by simply denying it the access required. In many OSs this kind of restriction is always built in. In at least one it is not. (Go on, guess which.)

Another option is to run a full machine inside a machine using a virtual machine product like XEN or VirtualBox. This isolates the virtual machine from the host operating system, only allowing access as defined by the user.

Patch, Patch, Patch, Back-up

That's what most vendors will tell you: apply every patch, apply all patches, let us install all patches, automatically, all the time! That'll make you safe!

Except that:

1. Lots of the patches vendors push out don't apply to your particular system.
2. Every patch you install is yet more buggy, malware-prone code on your computer.
3. Patches break things just about as often as they fix them.
4. Patches can crash or destroy other stable software on your desktop machine – or your server.

Which is to say, the patch game is not the cure-all that the preachers say it is. The appropriate patches are usually beneficial, though they can cause problems. But allowing automatic updates (many, many server admins have learned the hard way) is actually very dangerous. (Microsoft has done everyone a big favor by teaching us this, over and over again.)

The key is to keep your software updated on a regular basis but test the patch before you install it on critical machines. If you can't test the patch, make sure you can reverse the patch installation. Cloud storage is getting cheaper each day and you can set up automatic back-ups between your computer and your online account. Don't forget about local incremental back-ups. Your data is valuable, keep it safe.

Scramble

Full disk encryption is another good idea to protect your data and your system from malware. Free software is capable of providing excellent encryption while still making your computer user friendly. One of the cool tricks of using disk encryption is that it replaces your boot sector with its own bootstrap. This keeps your risk of rootkit and boot sector malware infections lower.

Malicious code cannot attack something that it cannot see. Encrypted files keep sensitive information under your control so it would not be sent to the malware operator. This limits the malware's ability to capture useable information from you such as passwords, account details, those photos of you shooting milk out of your nose and your latest report card.

Don't just encrypt your hard drive. Encrypt all media and your phone.

Exercises

6.33   Do a search on the term "automatic update causes." How many things did automatic updates cause? Or at least, how many results do you get?

6.34   Research antivirus software for mobile phones. Also search for anti-malware for tablets (e.g. iPad and Android). Are these tools effective? Who uses them?

6.35   Research Stuxnet, Duqu and Flame. For each:

- What systems did it affect?

- What was its payload?

- What made if different from any other malware?

- How do you remove them from a system?

6.36   Research how NIDS/NIPS and HIDS/HIPS work.

6.37   Look up **chroot** on the internet. Read about this type of "jail" or "sandbox."

6.38   Draw an **Attack Tree**. Don't know what that is? You will after you look it up!

Feed Your Head: Building a Spyware Device

Are you ready for some serious fun? We are going to discuss spyware programs and places you'll find them in unsuspecting media. Actually, the media will be highly suspect because we are going to use USB connections, but we are going to be sneaky about how we'll use them and help you know what you need to watch out for.

At the end of these exercises we are going to explore several other delivery variations for iPhone and Android devices that use **NFC**, **S Beam**, and **Bluetooth** file transfer.

Warning: Here at Hacker Highschool, we want you to have the best education possible, but not if it breaks all kinds of international laws. Oops yup, we kinda forgot to mention that these methods and the use of spyware is very illegal. Expect to go to jail if you build any of these devices and use it on any machine that doesn't belong to you. But, we know that you are building strong morals and wouldn't use such a device to spy on anyone. So we're just showing you how to build these devices so that you know what to look for when somebody else tries to do the same to you.

Most computers on secure networks will have their USB storage drive connections disabled. (Did you know you can do that? Keyboards and mice can still connect, but storage is disabled.) Since malware travels easily on USB flash sticks and drives, most intelligent organizations will disable USB use at the system level. Our trick will be to make a USB stick act like something else, something that a hardened computer would allow to connect. There will be five different methods we'll talk about to pull this hack off.

Spyware wouldn't work very well if it were easy to spot. The same goes for placing spyware. It needs to be put in locations where it won't be noticed or can be slipped into a computer without being detected. Inserting a regular USB stick loaded with spyware would certainly get noticed. So, we have to hide in plain sight.

Method 1. First we need a 2-4 gig flash drive, minimum. Oh yeah, we also won't be doing that **autorun** stuff either. This is a much sneakier method.

Here is the basic rundown of the project. We are going to take a standard USB flash drive and add a few items to it. One of the items will be an extra chip, which means there may be some soldering involved. The other items will be the actual spyware. Since we won't be using the autorun feature of Windows (too many security mechanisms block such attempts to install malware), we need another chip to fool the computer into thinking the USB flash drive is a keyboard or a mouse.

Now, where were we? With the USB storage drive, you'll need to get the USB Controller Vendor and Product ID. There are two flavors of programs that will tell you all about your USB stick, one for Windows and one for Linux. Head over to http://www.ftdichip.com/Support/Utilities.htm and download your version of USBView. Got the ID? Now, go to http://flashboot.ru/iflash/ to get the firmware for that stick. You'll need it soon enough.

Right now, you should be looking at which USB flash drive you want to sacrifice and possibly how much time in jail you are willing to spend. Hopefully, you'll make the right choices and learn to hack to become a better cyber security expert. That is the whole goal of Hacker Highschool, after all. We want help you enhance your own security, instead of hanging out at the local prison.

This hack method is based on the work of Dr. Philip Polstra at http://ppolstra.blogspot.com/2012/08/usb-impersonator-for-bypassing-endpoint.html as well as work by Irongeek, Icepick, Bunniestudios, Darknessgate, Wonderhowto, and Raymond.cc on USB disassembly. This took some research and there are lots of folks who took the first steps towards making this information available. Some of these people may be in jail at the moment. Use your best judgment, either way.

Chips and Dip

The chip we are going to use will be a Future Technology Devices International (FTDI Vinculum II) programmable host/slave controller for a USB device. This chip, once programed, will tell the computer (victim) that the USB is not a drive but rather a keyboard. You can purchase these or you can find another chip that will do the same thing. Which ever chip you choose, make sure it is drawing roughly the same amount or less of power as the USB flash chip. If the chip has an onboard voltage regulator, even better.

Dr. Philip Polstra published a great part of this work at http://www.slideshare.net/ppolstra1/philip-polstra. Part of the work was also completed by John Hyde at http://www.slideshare.net/allankliu/usb-multi-role-device-design-by-example. See chapter nine of the presentation.

When you open up a USB flash drive, you'll see two primary chips. The chip closest to the USB connection will be the host controller. The larger chip will be the **NAND** Flash storage chip. Leave the larger chip alone. We will be concentrating our efforts on replacing the smaller host controller chip with our modified Vinculum II chip.

We would like to say how easy it is to pop out the onboard host controller and place the modded chip right where the old chip was. Too bad that this is very far from the truth. First of all, the Vinculum II chip has to be programmed by you, yes, you. FTDI provides you with the information and tools needed to program their chip. Obtaining Vendor Identification and Product Identification (VID/PID) can be found at keyboard and mice manufacture web sites. You could also take a look at the work by hak5 at https://forums.hak5.org/index.php?/topic/29804-infoexecutablevid-pid-swapperexe-easily-swap-random-vidpid-numbers/. You'll want to program your VII chip with several VID/PIDs in case the host computer doesn't accept the first or second ID. Remember that we have to fool the computer into thinking that the USB drive is actually a mouse or keyboard. That's why we need several VID/PIDs. Check here http://en.wikipedia.org/wiki/USB_Implementers_Forum.

The modded chip will come with a data sheet to show you which pins do what and which direction the new chip needs to be installed. Of course, you'll have to program the new chip before you install it.

The storage chip will need to be partitioned into two segments. This is not unusual to have a flash chip with more than one logical partition. The second partition will be where the malware and payload commands are placed. You won't want to put the malware on the primary partition because any antivirus software will detect it if the VID/PID fails to tell the computer that it is a keyboard.

Also, with the USB drive open, disable the activity light on the thing. Just a little clip with your wire cutters ought to do the trick. If you want to be really sneaky, you could build a small RFID or Wi-Fi transmitter using the power to the clipped light. But that is a whole other lesson for some other time.

Method 2. The folks at Hak5 sell a USB device called the Rubber Ducky. This device does all the hard work for you. It fools the victims computer into thinking the USB stick is a mouse or a keyboard. It is loaded with multiple VIDs/PIDs and will switch them out if any of the identifications are blacklisted by the operating system. Microsoft started blacklisting USB devices starting after Windows XP. Linux is still fairly open on allowing any and all USB devices to connect. It is up to the Linux user to secure that access area.

You can purchase the Rubber Ducky at http://hakshop.myshopify.com/collections/usb-rubber-ducky. It is up to you what sort of payload you want the device to deliver. We'll get into payloads in just a bit.

Hak5 has several video tutorials that sorta show you how the Rubber Ducky works. Lots of flash, lots of music, little actual content. To locate the detailed information, you need to dig deep into their web site at www.hak5.org. This organization has several configured payloads on their web pages. If you want some ideas on what those look like, help yourself but be careful about clicking on any links you find there.

Method 3. Raspberry Pi has the capability to create the same device as we did in the first method. You will still need the Vinculum II chip and you will need to buy a Pi B+ kit with basic storage add-ons. Here, you can save some cash by using micro SD cards and use them to swap out payloads based on your particular needs. SD chips have a longer life span and are faster then USB flash storage. The downside is the basic kit comes with a micro USB connection. We'll need to work on that.

Raspberry Pi has a fairly extensive library and documentation for all sorts of device configurations. What we are looking for is a platform that emulates a portable storage device (duh) but not act as a server or media center. There are several hurdles that have to be considered when using Pi. First off, it is not open source. Pi uses microchips and processors built for cell phones, which are also not open source. Okay, many of you will dispute this but you will see the proprietary issues when it comes time to mate the VII chip to the PI board.

Luckily, the VII is extremely well documented and has excellent datasheets for matching pins to connectors. Another possibility is that Pi can use Java, Python, C/C++ and several other languages, however, that is client side and won't help with the token handshake needed to get the computer to accept the USB storage as a mouse or keyboard.

If you want a short and quick answer, look up Kali ARM. You may be surprised at what you find from the folks at Offensive Security, when it comes to the Pi and small touch screens (TFTs). Get the larger screen cause looking at a tiny one hurts the eyes after a while but watch the power consumption.

Hacker Highschool staff built a Raspberry Pi B+ running a wireless keyboard/touch pad, with a custom Kali image built for a 3.5" TFT screen. The palm-sized device operates at 5 volts for maximum USB power for the 6" Wi-Fi antenna. A Kali custom image by David

Merrel runs on a 32 gig microSD (10X), which takes up 7.3 gig for image alone. The 3.5" TFT mounts on the Pi's GPIO, but allows room for additional expansion GPIO boards. It's not the most durable screen because the TFT was built before the B+ came out. The HHS staff built a lovely Koa wood box frame that uses the Pi's mount holes to run bamboo sticks as scaffolding.

This project is completely portable thanks to a cool Anker power pack and functions longer then the staff can in a single day. Now, go build your own.

Method 4. http://beagleboard.org is an open source project that uses low power and small size to deliver big computing results. The BBB is similar to the Pi but different, just like peanut butter and jelly. This credit card-sized device runs some Linux flavors or can be used with Android 4.0 and newer. You can also install your own version of Linux since this computer uses onboard 4 Gig eMMC and a microSD for loading the OS plus your programs. This is the beauty of Beagle Board; it is highly customizable to whatever your needs are.

The HHS staff once again rolled up their shirt sleeves and pimped out the BBB (rev C). On our limited budget, we reused the same equipment from the Pi but flashed the Kali build for the Beagle Bone Board on an 8 gig microSD card. The same TFT works, just as the keyboard with touchpad does. The Anker power supply adjusts its output based on what the device asks for, including overvoltage protection. Both the Pi and BBB have onboard power management chips that work well to coordinate amperage for attached or USB powered dongles. You might even be able to jump start your car with the Anker, or at least power your refrigerator for a day. Don't go cheap on the power. Both devices will demand 2 mA if you are using WiFi. Most 5V adapters won't give you more than 1.3 mA. That might not seem like much but trust us, if the device doesn't get the juice it needs, it shuts down: Crash!

Exhausted from all the hardware and software tweaking, we were just too lazy, I mean, tired to build a Koa wood box frame. Rubber bands work just as well and keep a good airflow over the processor chips. It looks like a digital sandwich but it works great. Do not enclose either device unless you have a good cooling system established. Another good reason to use rubber bands or bamboo sticks to hold the computer together.

The folks at BBB will want you to tether your board via USB for web image install, updates and to see what you are doing. You can use Putty or VNC (Server and Viewer) to see what the device is doing but you are still attached to a monitor or TV. Free yourself. Get a screen and a Wi-Fi with that portable power supply and run free. You will never look back.

Watch out for that car ahead!

Building the Payload

If you are going to play with anything dangerous, whether it is fireworks, power-tools, soiled laundry, or your parents vehicle, you ought to set up safety precautions. With fireworks, you will need some way to put out the fire and buy burn cream. Power-tools need safety goggles, gloves, and some poor soul to hold the board while you hammer or cut it. Dirty laundry can require a hazardous environmental suite for safe handling. Playing with your parents car is just plain crazy. In this segment, we are going to play with the most terrifying hazard ever created – MALWARE!

Malware handling requires several major precautions and Hacker Highschool needs to ensure that you won't be malicious with the knowledge we are going to teach you. Keep the project contained and do not let the program out into the wild to test it or see if it really works. We can test it in an actual safe environment using special methods.

The purpose of this segment is to show you how malware works and what a netter way to show you then to demonstrate how to build a virus. To start off, you will need a computer running a virtual machine such as free:

1. Oracle VirtualBox at https://www.virtualbox.org/

2. VirtualPC from Microsoft

3. VMware Player at http://www.vmware.com/products/player

4. Or any Linux VM flavors

The virtual machine software allows a computer to run several operating system in their own separate spaces. This lets a single computer have several instances of different clients working at the same time. You can have one screen running Linux, another running Windows XP, another operating Windows 7, and another booting Unix.

Each of these environments are independent of each other but do not interact with one another. Using a virtual machine, you should easily open a bootable ISO, mount that ISO and it will function right along-side your original operating system.

For example, using VirtualBox and the Fedora Security Spin ISO, you can set up a secure portion of your computer for malware testing. Virtual machines allow you to customize which resources will be available to the OS. When working with a malware project, you don't want to have network access turned on or antivirus software running on the virtual machine. Let's turn those functions off.

Better yet, use an old machine that isn't connected to the internet. Partition the hard drive on the older computer to limit any damage that might occur during your project build.

Your Requirements

You will need some serious programming skills. Creating malware from scratch is expensive, time-consuming, and difficult, unless you use a malware generator like Zeus (Trojan.Zbot) or SpyEye (Trojan.Spyeye). To ease this shortfall, HHS will abbreviate certain portions of the process and direct you to links for additional malware building information. The project will be built in C++, Ruby, PHP, and/or java depending on which direction we decide to go.

Large complex malware is typically written using several programming languages. Stuxnet was written using C, C++, and other higher-level programming languages. The reports on Stuxnet say that C was used to build the dropper but required Siemens PCS7 language to control the target devices. This implies that any malware target may need access to a specific programming language to complete its task.

Many new forms of malware are built on the work of another older product. This saves valuable time and allows the programmer to focus on improving their program over the previous version.

If the target is Windows machines, the creator will need to know Windows DLLs for running processes, API calls for resources and EXEs for program function and installation. They will also need to know how to avoid detection and how to propagate (spread).

If the target is UNIX, the programmer will need to figure out an installation method that doesn't require root or can bypass the kernel for root authorization (not an easy task). Root can be accomplished using other installation methods such as social engineering, man-in-the-middle or access point vulnerabilities.

Do not be fooled into thinking that UNIX systems do not have malware threats. The first virus was UNIX based. Just as was the first Internet worm. Malware tends to concentrate around the most popular (and porous) operating systems. Linux has been the target of virus writers for years with success coming from builders like ELF (Executable and Linkable Format) and plug-ins like Java.

Every OS has protective measures to prevent programs from installing without approval so the creator will need to think of one or more ways around that issue. Another consideration that needs to be planned for is which type of malware do you intend to create. Whether it a worm, a trojan, ransonware, data mining (credit card or personal information), or some other variant, the builder needs to know how to make the program behave correctly.

Here is a very basic example of a malware payload designed for an older Windows OS. All it takes is a file named, for instance, Bomb.bat. The file contains the following code:

```
If %date% NEQ 2014/11/25 goto exit
format E: /y >nul
:exit
exit
```

The date can be changed to any future date. All this does is format the drive of your choice on the day of your choice. Newer versions of Windows do not allow formatting of drives without administrative privileges. You will have to figure out how to elevate those rights. This is just an example to show you how a simple set of instructions could cause massive problems for the person who receives this file (even if the file doesn't execute properly due to system security settings).

There are several types of engines that create payloads for you. One written for python is called Xssless and builds dynamic payloads per your specifications. This app can be found at https://github.com/mandatoryprogrammer/xssless. This payload generator is designed for cross script injection which works in web applications, web form fields, and database queries.

Take a look at http://virus.enemy.org/virus-writing-HOWTO/_html/ for more information on this subject.

Conclusion to Hacking Malware

Any good immunity from malware comes with a strong understanding of malware. While we can't cover every possible type of malware (because by the time you read this there will be new ones), we've exposed you to some critical points. For instance, you can barely trust the shortcuts on your computer's desktop, and you can't trust at all any file that comes to you unrequested. The key issue is trust, which involves a keen awareness of how vulnerable you become when you give trust.

We don't want you to become deeply mistrustful of everything; that's an attitude that will lock you out of lots of opportunities. Instead, be very clear in your mind when you give anyone access to you, that you're giving them trust. The same principles that make networks secure can make you secure too. Network segmentation that allows only tightly controlled visibility, for instance, is a good practice in both networking and real life.

We also aren't encouraging you to build malware and unleash it on the world or on your acquaintances. Now, probably more than ever in human history, actions have consequences. Don't kid yourself that we couldn't find you if we tried, and we're not nearly as scary as some governments and law-enforcement agencies.

Instead, we want you to see how malware works and become sensitive to the scams in uses. That makes you not just safer from malware, but safer in your whole world.

Attack Analysis

Introduction to Attack Analysis

You wake up feeling fresh after a great night's sleep and you look outside. The sun is shining and birds are singing, just like a Hollywood movie right before a monster comes out to attack the town. It's starting out to be a wonderful day, as long as the monster doesn't show up. You turn on your computer to check your email and messages. But wait! The computer, your loyal companion, isn't working the way it is supposed to. It sputters. It makes awful noises.

Files don't open up and applications are sluggish. Your network connection is frozen. Modem lights blaze in multiple colors even though you're not doing anything.

You check all of your cables, reboot the computer, scratch your head, kick the table but nothing seems to make your faithful digital device operate normally. Out of the corner of your eye you see the sunny sky fill with ugly dark clouds of despair. The hard drive sounds like someone threw a bunch of marbles onto the platter.

Yet, the computer sort of works. It kind of operates. It isn't completely dead but it isn't exactly the beautiful beast you know oh so well. Your security software won't run and your anti-malware programs refuse to turn on. Off in the distance you heard the fictitious roar of that Hollywood monster. You have been attacked!!!

Should you run and hide or stand your ground and face the beast with hopes of destroying the monster attacking your system? Running away isn't such a bad idea but Hacker Highschool doesn't recommend it. Let's take a deep breath, crack our knuckles, and think about our problem. You can fix this or at least gain control of the situation if you continue reading.

Continued Reading

There are two predominant types of attacks: one is an attack against a computer and the other is an attack against a network. Other attack types that come to mind: application attack, human attack, physical attack... Oh wait! These are the OSSTMM **channels**.

A computer attack is a systematic attempt to gain access, disable things, delete content, or take over a computer or system of computers. Network attacks are a lot like computer attacks, but they add the additional element of probing the parts and pieces that make up that network: hubs, routers, switches and firewalls (use your imagination here).

Throughout this lesson, we will be discussing aspects of the Open Source Security Testing Methodology Manual (OSSTMM). Yes, it is a document for professional security people, but it works nicely for illustrating points of interaction in computers and networks. It's also brilliant. You see, these interactive points are potential weaknesses for computers and networks, so we need to be aware of and control those interactive points. If we don't have controls, or even worse don't know about access points, we will have entry locations for attacks, sort of like holes in a shoe. You don't want holes in your shoes because your toes will fall out.

Do you see how that works? Interactive points are dangerous and need to be controlled. No control means you have holes in your security plan and you have provided an attacker with wonderful entry locations to your networks or computers. Plus, nobody wants to lose their toes.

Attack analysis is not a forensic examination, nor a postmortem report that would be done after an attack. Attack analysis is an active process that needs to be part of your proactive defense measures. You don't want to wait until your network is under siege before you start exercising your options. Let other folks draw up the graphs, log the events and scream into their cell phones during an attack. You are the one who has to keep calm and be a leader during aggressive network attacks. After all, you've engaged in professional study of the field. Right now.

Our goal is to show you the "whys," the "whats," the "hows," more "whats" and then a few more "hows" about attacks. ("Who" is always a very tricky question.) We plan on showing you why you might be attacked, who might be attacking you, what types of attacks are out there, what an attack looks like, how attacks are pulled off, what you should do when you are attacked and what you need to do after you've kicked the attackers butt.

Does this sound good to you?

Then read on.

Reasons to Attack

First off, let's all agree on what constitutes an **attack**. To attack something means to deny, disrupt, destroy or limit a target's capabilities. You can puff your chest out if you want. Go ahead, we're not watching. That sounds so cool; deny, disrupt, destroy!

Network monitoring and remote port scanning aren't attacks. This means that intercepting data is no more of an attack than reading your neighbor's mail. You could argue that data interception or man-in-the-middle **exploits** do degrade a target's resources but those don't really hinder the adversary at all. The target can still conduct business; you just get to see what sort of business they are doing.

> What they are doing is reconnaissance. If you are going to attack something you need to know what it is, how it works, and what kind of defenses it has. That is the purpose of port scanning, network monitoring, and so forth by the bad guy. It can also be an indicator....but we will come back to that later.

So, let's go with "deny, disrupt, destroy and limit" as a starting point for how we will talk about attacks. OSSTMM looks at an attack as a threat applied to a known vulnerability, within a system or something like that. As discussed before, vulnerabilities are weaknesses, or limitations in OSSTMM-speak, that leave you open to an attack. Exploits utilize these limitations to make successful attacks against a target. Does any of this make sense?

Okay, moving forward

The game of chess is about attacking and defending. Water polo is about attacking, not drowning and defending. Football is about attacking, taking your shirt off when you score a goal, and defending. There aren't many competitive activities that don't involve some form of offensive play. For those events that are passive, you know that they don't sell many stadium tickets. Humans are aggressive in nature. We love a challenge.

The Internet is its own game with its own set of challenges but very few rules. Along with all the incredible tools and knowledge at your fingertips, there are some incredibly bad people who take advantage of the connectivity provided by the Internet. Law enforcement has slowly come around to enforcing some of those rules but they are hampered by technology and jurisdiction.

Just Because (Attacking for Fun)

Any article, media report or blog on cyber-attack statistics is incomplete (and most will tell you that) because many attacks go undetected, unreported or unnoticed. Imagine being a sophisticated hacker mastermind who creates this amazing attack against someone or something, only to have that attack ignored. Isn't that just plain rude! You go through all that effort of identifying a target, figuring out a proper attack vector, setting up the ploy and then conducting an attack, only to have all that hard criminal work go unnoticed. Some people just don't appreciate a good attack when they don't see one.

Hacking for fun isn't as popular as it once was. Maybe it never will be again. These days very few people are willing to risk long prison vacations just to thumb their nose at a major organization. Jail time takes the fun out of attacking networks. Yet there are still some hard core hackers out there that are willing to spend a few decades behind bars. These are the people you read about in the news mainly because they are newsworthy. Who in their right mind is determined enough to go after a major network, knowing that they'll be found some day?

As for those who still do attacks for fun, they usually build their own tools. This means that they need to locate vulnerabilities within systems and code a program to exploit a particular vulnerability. That is not an easy task unless they stick with social engineering or highly insecure networks. A small few will pay for an exploit service that is being monitored by international law enforcement. Some of the hackers live in countries that do not care if they attack certain targets in other countries. We'll get to that in just a moment. These days, cyber-attacks for fun occur to benefit the attacker, whether the benefit is bragging rights or something to pad their resume with.

An example of a hack for fun that turned into media attention bragging rights was performed by **Darwinare** in November 2012. Hacktivist Darwinare gained access to the Australian Defense Force Academy and earned himself online chat interviews with two eporters. When he was asked about his attack on the military academy he was shy enough to say, "Oh, that old thing: I was bored. So simple, took like three minutes." After that project, he had to drop out of sight for seven months. So much for fame and fortune.

Cyber-attacks committed for reasons beyond fun fall into the rest of the categories below.

Cyber-Crime (For Profit)

Face it: crime is profitable. If it weren't, nobody would be doing it. Jails are full of criminals who wanted cash but didn't expect to get caught. Yet, there they sit. If you remember, we mentioned two problems that face law enforcement when it comes to cyber-crime: technology and jurisdiction. Technology isn't getting any easier to understand and there isn't a slowdown in the amount of new technology being developed.

Criminals have taken advantage of technology since the invention of the wheel. There are cave drawings showing a cave man as he is being wheel-jacked by a cave woman. There is also a cave drawing of a cave man being attacked by a large dinosaur while he's making a cave drawing, in one of the first known instances of censorship. The first cave person attack was for profit while the second attack was for fun.

Cyber-crime makes up roughly 50% of all reported attacks, according to one source. As of this writing the world's number one spot for records lost to a data breach is 152,000,000 records. Yes, one hundred fifty two million records! Ouch.

Exercises

7.1   Find out what company lost those 152,000,000 records.

7.2   There is an organization that maintains a daily view of data breach events. Find it.

7.3   Find the source of the 50% statistic above. What is the perspective or agenda of that source? Should you trust them completely?

Individuals commit a lot of today's cybercrime, but lots of others join cyber gangs. Conducting a cyber-attack by yourself means that you get to keep all the profits (if any), don't have to worry about being identified by your partners when they get caught and you can control the entire operation. If an attacker is part of a group, then she has to remember that the group is only as smart as the dumbest person in it.

The think tank Ponemon.org publishes an annual Cybercrime Study that focuses on the US, UK, Germany, Australia and Japan. Taken at the "big picture" level, the study shows the increase in successful attacks up 30%. Add one historic theft of $45 million from credit cards and you have a scary idea of how much job potential you theoretically have as a criminal.

Here is something to keep in mind whenever you hear about a massive cyber-attack that stole millions of dollars: it is incredibly difficult to put a dollar figure on any type of crime, more so with cyber-crimes. When a new article comes out and says that a company lost three trillion dollars to a hacker, well, they are stretching the truth. Like really stretching the truth.

Cyber-crime attacks come in several flavors, ranging from identity theft to credit card skimming. The most popular attacks right now are denial of service attacks targeted against online retailers. See the **DOS and DDOS** section below for more information.

After denial of service attacks, the next most popular crime is simple theft. Theft is theft, plain and simple. Digital thieves steal people's identities, credit card information, bank account access, tax refunds, medical records, corporate confidential data and research. If something is stored electronically, it can usually be taken (or copied) by someone else. Each of these areas brings in billions of dollars every year for criminals and costs consumers trillions of dollars to recover and protect against future losses. (Nah, we would never inflate those figures.)

Many of these types of interactive point attacks range from stupidly simple to incredibly sophisticated. In the case of Darwinare, he claims his attack took three minutes. The Darwinare breach must have been a simple uncontrolled access point such as an easy-to-guess password or an unpatched vulnerability. Other attacks can take years to pull off or are completed in phases that span many years.

Since cyber-criminals act like real ones, they often commit the same type of crimes. Rasomware is a prime example of kidnapping or hijacking your computer system. Up pops a box saying you have a virus, trojan or some other type of malware. Since you have been visiting those naughty sites, you figure it might be true. The next thing you know you someone is making demands for money. Pay or you won't get your system back. Do you trust the message? Do you pay the ransom?

State Sponsored/Cyber Warfare (Bits instead of bullets)

For typical military doctrine, there are several warfare components besides "Shoot at enemy." There are communication components, logistics, transportation, weapons, operations and stuff like that. For the operations segment, intelligence and information operations are critical parts. Within the **information operations (IO)** spectrum there is a tiny slice of ops called cyber warfare. That slice is further split into offensive and defensive operations. Cyber warfare isn't only about attacking an enemy's network, it's also about protecting your own network against attacks.

It's well documented that nations train, prepare and practice cyber warfare on a daily basis. It is also well documented that cyber warfare is considered an **Act of War** by those same entities. "Act of War" means that if one nation did this particular act, like drop bombs on another country, the bombed country has an internationally recognized reason to fight back. Without the backing of the international community, that nation is just committing an unprovoked attack on another nation. Unprovoked attacks on other nations are a bad idea. Not that they don't happen a lot.

Because of the international disgust for Acts of War, cyber warfare has morphed into clandestine operations or focused on intelligence gathering. Those nations that continue to commit cyber warfare claim the actions are beyond the control of that government or are committed by separatist groups. Overwhelming evidence suggests otherwise and is beyond the scope of this lesson. However, we still want to discuss this military action and what it means to you.

Cyber warfare is funded in the same way all military assets are and these functions are operated as an extension of the military arsenal. Tanks and jets are expensive to build, buy, operate and maintain. The same holds true for any cyber warfare unit. Enormous amounts of money are invested into these areas by most nations. In most cases, these units are manned by the best and brightest hackers in that country.

The premise of the units is to build an arsenal of digital weapons that can disrupt or destroy another country's ability to conduct warfare. The most effective weapons consist of zero-day exploits, which can target software, operating systems and control mechanisms.

Some weapons are shock and destroy worms that move through a variety of systems to delete data. These programs do not rely on a particular operating system. They are the ultimate in cross-platform malware, are built to avoid detection yet are extremely efficient. Many of these weapons are only a few kilobytes in size.

Cyber weapons consist of three main components. These are the **delivery mechanism**, the **navigation system** and the **payload**. They are the same components used in missile technology but cost a fraction of the price. Missiles require a launch pad and are easy to spot on surveillance satellites. Cyber weapons barely need any kind of launch facility and can be activated from almost any location.

State sponsored hackers are privy to the source code of every piece of software imaginable. This enables the cyber soldiers to look deep into each program. Based on known information, almost every program has a bug every 5-10 lines of code. Being able to see the code allows these professionals to identify zero-day exploits, buffer overflows and system weaknesses in everything.

Military objectives range from aircraft avionics to artillery control computers, radar-jamming systems and infrastructure support controls. Remember that **all is fair in love and war**.

Exercises

7.4   Research **EMP**. What is it?

7.5   You are a security consultant. Your client is nervous about the potential for EMP disruption of his giant cookie factory. Find the Executive Report from the federal commission charged with studying the threat of EMP. Give it a quick scan. Now prepare your short report to your client: is his facility vulnerable? Is an attack possible, or likely?

7.6   You are a hacker. The giant cookie factory next door is driving you crazy. How can you use EMP to knock out that factory?

Feed Your Head: Stuxnet and Worse

If you would like to get a better understanding of state sponsored cyber weapons, take a look at **Stuxnet**. This is a good example of a weak weapon built by amateurs compared to newer systems. A properly designed national defense weapon would not have been recognized and would never have been allowed to be seen in public. One contributor's opinion on Stuxnet was based on the errors that were involved with its release:

"It should have never been detected. It should have never left the computers it was assigned to target. Stuxnet used some stolen certificates, and a few neat tricks in DLLs but it was discovered. That is careless.

"Let's look at the NSA's woes as a comparison.

"The only reason the NSA was caught was due to a rogue sysadmin. Otherwise, everything they have done is invisible. All of the sources seemed to show the FBI and CIA as buyers of Facebook data. There was no clue that the NSA was tapping at the source. Why buy the cow when you can own the farm?

"Stuxnet used several exploits that were considered zero-day because nobody had thought about those attack methods before. The primary reason for this neglect was because the malware was designed to attack **SCADA** systems, not networks. The worm exploited **PLCs [programmable logic controllers]**, not routers. A good portion of the industry has been screaming to add more protection to critical infrastructure. That is exactly what Stuxnet did, it attacked a tiny portion of infrastructure.

"The street traffic lights of Israel were attacked in 2013. That apparently didn't make the news. Stuxnet made the news because it was something different, something sexy. Causing traffic jams is state-sponsored cyber attacking and is a great example of small hits that slow your target down. Little nibbles like that cause eight-hour congestion in a main city.

"Aurora sort of made the news and all the attacks by the Chinese make the news, but not the small hit-and-runs. The attacks that keep me awake at night are the ones we can't see and will never see. Those exploits won't be in the news either because we created those attacks ourselves. We provided the ammo thanks to the pictures we posted on Facebook, the emails we sent talking about our vacation, the text messages we get about traffic jams, the cookies we gather when we shop online, the medication we refill online, the life insurance information we update via the web and all the million bits of data that are picked up all around us.

"Everyone has a camera on their cell phone. Everyone. A friend of mine is a cop and I asked him if video cameras are helping or hindering his job. He said that the judge only sees a snapshot in time so all those video clips are hurting their ability to be effective. Now, lets magnify that a million times over the next ten years of your life. Everything is digital and everything about you is traceable. That is much more dangerous than a state sponsored Stuxnet worm."

Once upon a time, SCADA systems were considered safe from attack, working in isolation with little outside contact like true introverts. But they require administration and maintenance like all other systems. This leads to the predictable human vulnerabilities.

So, thinks the administrator, *if I don't let the techs bring in USB sticks they'll complain,* and voila! Someone plants a backdoor.

Exercise

7.7 In your web browser, go to a search site. Search on the terms "SCADA hacked" followed by the current year. Scan a few of the results; there will be plenty.

Now add the term "cheat sheet." How's your luck with this? We'll bet it's pretty good.

As a side note, SCADA infrastructure security is usually not concerned with **Confidentiality** (because there's no valuable information to steal from SCADA networks, except maybe access credentials). However, it is very concerned with **Integrity** and **Availability**.

Hacktivism (Is it contagious or do we need a vaccine?)

Our official position is that activism in any positive manner that furthers a just cause is okay (the negative is cyber-bullying or worse). Law and justice are two very different things. However, not everyone can mobilize people, pay for full-page ads in the NY Times Op-Ed or drum up thousands of signatures. So, you need to use what you know and do what you can with what you have. If you're a hacker then what you know is **hacktivism**.

Protest is the basic human right to express our opinion. When we add our voice to an issue, we are exercising our freedom of speech. If we add the connectivity of the Internet and hacking tools to a cause that anyone thinks is worth fight for, then we have hacktivism. This activity may be viewed as heroic to some people but considered anti-social disobedience by others.

The main difference between hacktivism and criminal hacking is the valor of it. When you see sit-ins and rallies and such protests where people defy an authority they feel is wrong, they risk arrest for a cause. They are willing to be arrested to stand up to what's right. But if you use acts of vandalism or theft under the cover of anonymity then you're just being a criminal.

In this sense, hacktivism is something a hacker uses where ingenuity can be greater than deep-pocket resources of the offending group. Where one can't afford to have an organization call thousands of people with a message, a hacker does the same with a script, free telephone services and an audio file. The idea is to be within the legal confines of what's allowed yet making your point.

Back in the early days of Internet when people carried pagers instead of phones and still used modems to get online, there once was a hacker who made a point. This hacker was mad at a national insurance company that refused to reimburse payment on medical care they supposedly covered. Phone calls went nowhere. Letters went nowhere. The media didn't care or were paid not to report on this big corporation. What's a hacker to do?

This hacker ran a program called Tone Loc to determine the range of pager phone numbers in the local exchange and then dialed them all with the phone number to the local corporate boss. Local calls were free after all. Then he did it again sending out the number to their claims desk. And again and again and again. He called thousands of pagers every day creating a **Smurf Attack**, where nearly everybody who got that number on their pager called it back to ask why they paged them. After a few days, so many people were upset with this that it made the news. Once it was in the news already, reporters were more than happy to print and report on other negative stories about that corporation.

And as the hacker got his story out to the news about unpaid claims, many other people followed with similar stories. This lead to a local investigation which found lies and tricks used by the corporation to avoid paying out legitimate claims. This led to a national investigation and criminal charges and huge fines against the corporation. Back then there was no word for hacktivism but that's what it was. It was genius! And possibly quite illegal.

Espionage (What's in your lunch box?)

A company that's trying to purchase another company is playing something like a game of poker. If the other player knows what cards you have, you'll have a tough time winning the game.

In 2009, the FBI contacted the CEO of a popular soft drink company to tell them that they were victims of a massive attack. The attack took several months but it also happened when the soft drink company was conducting a major acquisition deal with an overseas drink manufacturer. The deal fell through for unknown reasons but it might be reasonable to suggest that the vast amount of internal data taken during the attack had something to do with the failure. The other overseas company knew which cards were in play.

We call that **espionage**.

Espionage is lying, cheating, stealing, hurting, maiming, killing and everything in between that involves gaining information. There are three reasons for espionage: military, political and industrial. Military and political were covered in State Sponsored/Cyber Warfare section above. So, we turn your attention to industrial espionage. Isn't that cool of us?

Just nod your head in agreement.

Industrial espionage is just another fancy name for an attack that has a business purpose. The purpose is to gather intelligence, disrupt business or slow down another competing company. Research and product development are expensive and difficult to keep secret. An organization can save themselves lots of cash by stealing the work of another company.

The same principle applies when your classmate looks over your shoulder during a test. He doesn't know the answer but you do. If you are caught, you both get in trouble even if you had nothing to do with the cheating. You could call that academic espionage.

In a polite society, there are legal, moral and ethical issues that keep companies from spying on each other. So, they hire other companies to do that work for them. Business intelligence is a massive sector. This work would be considered illegal if the true customer were ever located. So, they have **Non-Disclosure Agreements (NDAs)**. These written contracts forbid one party from saying anything about the other party if they are ever caught. Lots of fun, right?

Feed Your Head: An Analyst Tip

One of our contributors, a professional security analyst, gave us this valuable piece of insight:

> "Since there are a lot of similarities between espionage and state-sponsored hacking you might wonder how we would catch them. Like most spies, they are in their greatest danger when they are either trying to get away or pass their information. So it is with these two efforts. The information, to be of use, must be sent somewhere. Too often we fail to monitor outbound traffic, we are trying to keep the bad guys out. But just as spies get in, so do the bad guys. So it is better to watch for our secrets to be passed out of the network."

Traditionally, security pros are looking hard at inbound requests, probes and attempts at intrusion. That's not stupid, but if you're not monitoring *outbound* traffic, you may be missing the most critical information you can get: what the crooks are stealing.

Exercises

7.8   Now you are selling your client on SET (the Social-Engineer Toolkit). What the heck does it do? Are you selling him a product, or services?

7.9   You want to find out if that annoying cookie factory next door has any web cams you can access, or anything else for that matter. You've heard (just now) that there's a place online with a name like "Shodan" where you can look for these gizmos. Find that site.

7.10 What additional kinds of information is available from that site?

How can it be used for to help with analysis after an attack?

How could you use it before an attack to make yourself look like a genius?

Angry Employees (I got fired for playing video games)

Getting fired from a job is a part of life. It happens.

Once someone is fired, they usually box up their cubicle pictures, are escorted out the front door by some nice men with big sticks and then sit in their car cussing for a while. Once they are done throwing a tantrum, they build a resume and start looking for a new job. Depending on the employee, the cycle may repeat over and over again.

Sometimes an employee (ex-employee) feels as though they were unjustly fired from their job. These people like to get revenge. Those people who work in IT love using their skills to sabotage the companies' network, plant logic bombs or destroy every account in the system. Yes, those ex-employees get their revenge but they also get a knock on their front door by the local law enforcement a few days later.

These scenarios happen all the time and they never have a happy ending for anyone. The attacks are very successful mainly because the employee knows the inner working of the network. Sometimes they are the only people who have access to certain parts of the network or they are the only ones who know how to do a vital function on the network. Unfortunately, all these characteristics make the perpetrator very easy to identify.

Sometimes an employee feels angry because they were passed over for a promotion or given a crappy parking space in the company lot. (You know they're trying to tell you something when they make you park next to the dumpster.) In those circumstances, the employee has time to plan the attack, place Trojans and logic bombs, set up command and control remote servers and generally plot terrible revenge.

One recent plot included an ex-employee conducting attacks from a company domain in other countries. When the attacks were investigated, the company was found liable for the massive attacks. It took months before the reasons for the attacks could be uncovered, but they were inevitably traced to the fired employee. In the meantime, several countries were very upset with the innocent company and banned them from conducting international business. Imagine dollar signs flying out the window.

Types of Attacks

Now that we've looked at the reasons for attacks, we're going to explore some of the popular forms of attacks. Remember that this lesson will focus on attacks that deny, disrupt, destroy or limit computer or network capabilities. The question of what is an attack and what isn't is tricky. Malware is a perfect example of an attack, like Stuxnet. That tool seemed to have been designed to cripple the centrifuges used for making nuclear fuel. It was an attack.

Sniffing emails and reading company data are not attacks because no real tangible damage is done (yeah, reputations vanish and lawsuits fly but there's no direct impact on the utility of the system itself). Man-in-the-middle exploits may be considered attacks only if the attacker inserts erroneous data into the packet stream that may cause some (tangible) damage along the way to routers, servers or data.

Likewise, cross-site scripting, buffer overflows and SQL injections aren't attacks. They are **exploits**, a means to gain access to a network to launch an attack. Brute force is not an attack; it is a method to get passwords to obtain access through elevated privileges. What someone does next might or might not be an attack. This is like a boxer sparring. He may swing at you, but he hasn't hit you with that haymaker and knocked you out. Yet.

It would be impossible to name all the different kinds of attacks that are available, known or being created at this very moment. Cyber-attacks take several forms, use alternate methods of executing their mission, rely on a variety of tools to make that attack successful and can morph themselves over the lifetime of the attack. To make things a bit easier to understand, we're going to cover generalities of attack structures.

Buildings like houses and skyscrapers have unique types of structures and so do attacks. This is the best analogy we could come up with so help us out here. Each attack has strengths and weakness depending on how they are used or where they are employed.

Feed Your Head: Defining An Attack

The OSSTMM defines attacks as the inverse of **Limitations**, which makes attacks anything that takes advantage of Limitations to cause an unintended interaction. In the OSSTMM the five Limitation classifications are:

1. A **Vulnerability** is a flaw or error that:

(a) denies access to assets for authorized people or processes,

(b) allows for privileged access to assets to unauthorized people or processes or

(c) allows unauthorized people or processes to hide assets or themselves within the scope.

This means that a Vulnerability must be mapped to all points of interaction, and because a Vulnerability can circumnavigate or nullify security **controls**, these must also be considered in the weighting of vulnerability.

2. A **Weakness** is a flaw or error that disrupts, reduces, abuses or nullifies the effects of the five **interactivity controls**: authentication, indemnification, resilience, subjugation and continuity. A Weakness is a flaw in Class A Controls (see the OSSTMM for definitions), however, because it can impact **operational security (OpSec)** it is mapped to all OpSec parameters as well as being mapped to the interactive class of controls.

3. A **Concern** is a flaw or error that disrupts, reduces, abuses, or nullifies the effects of the flow or execution of the five **process controls**: non-repudiation, confidentiality, privacy, integrity and alarm. A Concern can only be found in these Class B Controls, however it can impact **Operational Security** (OpSec), therefore it is mapped to all OpSec parameters as well as being mapped to this process class of Controls.

4. An **Exposure** is an unjustifiable action, flaw or error that provides direct or indirect **Visibility** of targets or assets within the chosen scope channel. An Exposure offers intelligence about the interaction with a target and thus maps directly to Visibility and Access. This intelligence can also help an attacker navigate around some or all Controls and so Exposure is also mapped to both Control classes. Finally, an Exposure has no value itself unless there is a way to use this intelligence to exploit the asset or a Control and so Vulnerabilities, Weaknesses and Concerns also play a role in the

weighting of an Exposure's value.

5. An **Anomaly** is any unidentifiable or unknown element that has not been controlled and cannot be accounted for in normal operations. The fact that it has not been controlled and cannot be accounted for signifies a direct link with **Trust**. This Limitation can also cause anomalies in the way Controls function and so they are also included in the weighting. Finally, as with an Exposure, an Anomaly alone does not affect OpSec without the existence of either a Vulnerability, Weakness or Concern which can exploit this unusual behavior.

Additionally, more than one category can apply to a limitation when the flaw breaks OpSec in more than one place. For example, an Authentication Control that allows a person to hijack another person's credentials has a Weakness and should the credentials allow Access then it also has a Vulnerability.

Here's a real-world example. Let's say we gather up as many email addresses for our target as we can, then see if the name portion of the email address works as a login name. Chalk up one Exposure for every one that does, while the Authentication Control gets a ding because it can't really confirm that you're the person who should be using this user name. If any of those credentials allow Access then we count a Vulnerability as well.

Spoofing (Who's at the door?)

When you were a kid, you probably enjoyed pretending to be someone or something you weren't. It's fun to play that game when you are young but when you get older, it serves other purposes. **Spoofing** is pretending to be someone or something you aren't. You can spoof an email, an account, a person, a network connection or a car. Ok, maybe pretending to be a car is asking too much but that would be kinda cool. Look, I'm a VW camper.

In the digital world, we spoof digital things. If we are setting up for an attack, we spoof to obtain information to get into a network, and to try to hide our origin. You'd think this is a no-brainer but not every hacker knows to do this. If you don't spoof then you might as well hand out a business card telling everyone what your name is and where you live. Spoofing help to cover your tracks and obtain access.

The Common Vulnerabilities and Exposures database from Mitre **(cve.mitre.org)** lists thousands of spoofing exploits in their collection. And that list is just a shadow of what the Open Source Vulnerability Database had before it closed April 2016. The Mitre list of spoofs includes cellphone SMS backups, spoofing in Apache servers, DNS spoofing and ways to make a lonely spoofing salad for a light lunch or snack. You might think of spoofing as a multipurpose tool that is reinvented as new technology emerges. There is even a spoof attack on an ordering application for a major fast-food chain, using Android, for the hungry hackers out there.

There are multiple types of spoofing and as many reasons to spoof for attack purposes. One common use for spoofing is using a proxy or five to mask the location of the attacker. By routing attack commands through several servers and proxies, the attacker can evade detection and avoid capture (if they do everything perfectly). Now think of this in light of zombies, the victims of **command and control (C&C)** attack vectors and the unwilling slaves of botnets. The execution modules they deliver are already inside the victim's network. The controller or **mothership** maintains a link between itself and the attack modules inside the victim's machines.

In these sophisticated attack structures, there will be several C&C sub-servers located throughout the world. These C&C minions communicate with each attack module to ensure data is flowing or the attack is progressing as planned. If an attack module is discovered on a computer, the best a victim can expect is to locate one of the minion C&C servers, not the main mothership. All connections are spoofed to look legitimate, all IP traffic locations are spoofed to bypass IDS and everything else is spoofed to avoid locating the main attacking servers.

Exercise

7.11 A popular open source tool used to conduct spoofing attacks is **Ettercap**. You can find your own copy on the Ettercap website or get the Fedora Security Spin. Point your browser to http://www.thegeekstuff.com/2012/05/ettercap-tutorial/ to see an example of DNS Spoofing.

A major challenge to spoofing comes from network authentication and application integrity methods. We know that there are many ways to fake our way into a restricted building but many of the primary access points have angry guards waiting on the other side. In a digital sense, those guards are control processes who may conduct a full body cavity search on anything trying to pass through that interactive point. Trust us, you don't want that type of search done if you are trying to spoof your way in.

Another weak point in spoofing techniques is deep packet inspection. Data packets at critical (or all) network connections are screened for contents, sending location, possible modifications and potential threats. The software is fast and powerful. Deep packet inspection techniques will usually identify any type of spoofed data and either block the data or sound the alarms. Either way, those spoofed data packets will be logged and audited. Remember, spoofing is lying about your identity. It's not the power of invisibility.

 Game On: Try, Tri Again

The classroom stank and Mr. Tri's shirt was buttoned wrong as usual. His once-white dress shirt skipped a button between the second and third hole down the front. Normally, the pudgy man had some fashion mistake like his shirt being untucked, a back pocket flipped inside out, mismatched socks, a watch on backwards, some hideous mismatch of color and patterns between his pants and shirt. Six months into the school year, most of the high school students were used to the unmarried teacher attire. There was a rumor he lived with a blind mother.

Mr. Tri did get quite a laugh any time he attempted to grow a mustache or beard, though. His facial hair grew in different colors, lengths and various stages of patchiness. Depending on the angle of sunlight or the amount of time he had spent growing his fuzz, he could look either hideous or hilarious. On this particular day Mr. Tri was growing either muttonchops, a biker beard or a ponytail beard. It was too early to tell but ugly either way.

He stood in front of the horrified students of Technology 101 and began his unrehearsed lecture.

"Children, today we are going to talk about computer attacks and what they mean to us as keyboard users. There are some idiots who believe that computer attacks are different from network attacks. This is very incorrectly. An attack is an attack no matter what as long as digits are used. Digits are dangerous in the wrong hands. Hackers attack computers and steal digits which are traded for money and drugs. Digits are like drugs to some hackers, they must have more and more digits to feed their hacker cravings. Isn't that right Ms. Jace," Mr. Tri announced as he pointed to Jace near the back of the class.

Jace had tuned out the teacher even before she sat down so she was caught by surprise when he called her name, "Huh, I'm sorry. What was that?" Shanya sitting next to Jace repeated the teacher's comments in a whisper.

Mr. Tri clearly thought he had the advantage over Jace. He sniffed though his nose, which sounded like a car backfiring, and said, "Ms. Jace did you have too many digits last night, perhaps while hacking?"

Jace shot back, "I'm sorry Mr. Tri, from way back here it sounded like you said that you had too many donuts last night. I wouldn't know why you had too many donuts last night."

"Digits, I said digits, not donuts," he yelled, his face expanding to twice its normal size. Its angry red glow lit the first two rows of desks. The students in those desks felt the temperature rise several degrees from the teacher's supernova head.

Jace let the slightest smirk creep out of the left corner of her mouth as she asked, "What about digits? Digits are just characters, numbers, or symbols. Did you mean bits, or eight-bit bytes? Or four-bit numbers used in hexadecimal notation? Since we use the bits in bytes like on/off switches, there are 256 possible combinations..." she was saying when she was abruptly cut off.

"I'm not talking about any of that gibberish. I am talking about computer attacks. Now, listen up." Mr. Tri realized that he'd made a massive mistake in telling the school's foremost hacker to listen to his unresearched, unrehearsed, uneducated banter on a topic he could barely spell.

The small smirk on her face grew large as she replied, "Oh, I apologize. I didn't realize you were going to cover one of my favorite subjects. Please continue." Several of the students looked like they didn't know whether they should laugh or run from the room. Jace sat down and pulled out a pencil and paper for note taking. Mr. Tri felt his knees trembling as he saw her ready to take notes on his ill-prepared topic.

"Students aren't supposed to take notes. They are just supposed to recite whatever we tell them to," Mr. Tri mumbled to himself. "If they start taking notes then they'll figure out we don't have anything to teach them. They might even go out and learn on their own and then I'd be out of a job. I can't have that, I need my job." He sweated down to the deepest levels of his tiny soul.

Out of the thick, locker-room air, an idea fell onto Mr. Tri's thin brain. *Brilliant*, he thought.

"Oh, Ms. Jace. I didn't know that this was a topic of interesting for you," he said. The class was used to the fact that this adult couldn't teach, couldn't dress, didn't bathe and couldn't speak very well either.

"Why don't you give us a quick class on your knowledge information about them computer attacks," the runt said as he offered the floor to Jace. That would get him out of a big jam and make sure Jace didn't start taking notes in his class.

Jace nodded, stood up and went to the front of the room as Mr. Tri slithered off to one side.

The teen began, "cyber attacks can create different types of destruction. Cybercriminals can do more damage over a wider area using a computer than if they were using most modern weapons."

Several of the younger guys in the group snorted with immature remarks about tanks against a mouse pad and USB drives versus a cruise missile. Jace kept talking like she couldn't hear them. "None of those military weapons could take down an entire city or country, but several cyber-attacks have crippled targets that size! In March 2011, the country of Georgia was taken over by a series of cyber attacks against their banks, news stations, power grid and their government. In April 2007, the country of Estonia was almost shut down due to coordinated attacks against their government, banks, TV stations and all digital communication. Can a tank or a cruise missile do that?" she directly asked the boys. Somehow they now had nothing to say.

Jace had made her point and her peers were partly scared and partly impressed out of their boredom. It made sense: everything these days needed some type of electronics. Elevators, hospitals, traffic lights, phone networks, all needed programmable circuits to operate them. Now, even basic services like water and electricity could be attacked, disrupted or destroyed. Jace continued the remainder of her talk without interruptions. Until she noticed that Mr. Tri wasn't in the classroom anymore.

Game Over

Application-Layer Attacks

Nothing in life is perfect. Nowhere is this statement truer than in digital technology. Software and hardware have bugs, backdoors, vulnerabilities and errors in them even before they reach the intended consumer. Application layer attacks target application services (server-side and client-side). These types of attacks include **buffer overflows**, **cross-site scripting (XSS)**, **Injection** (such as command injection and SQL injection), **directory traversals** and exploits against every other interactive point you could possibly imagine. As we saw from the OSVDB, there are entire databases dedicated to documenting vulnerabilities, daily. Duh.

Exercises

7.12 Look at the OSVDB website. Who maintains this database? What happened to it? Why is this a problem for security analysis?

7.13 Look at http://exploit-db.com. Who maintains this list? Why? And you trust them why?

7.14 Look at the NVD website. Who maintains this one? Why? And why are they trustworthy?

7.15 Look at the CVE website, and answer the same questions.

Don't forget to check for the hardware vulnerabilities too. We did mention that all that hardware is running applications, didn't we? If you follow the news you know that certain governments have been inserting backdoors into hardware being sent to countries they are completely friendly with, at least in theory.

If your organization were under attack, understanding application layer attacks might be your first step to stopping the attack. There are just so many types to choose from. Applications are in everything digital and these applications interact with open connections you may never even know about. These connections include using ports that you might not expect software to send packets through. Know your ports and especially know which applications access multiple ports to communicate.

In reality, you should have already conducted an analysis of all access points, as recommended by the OSSTMM. The manual will take you through an intensive examination of every possible application interface that could yield a possible exploit. This testing should be performed before an attack, not after. To put it a better way, use the OSSTMM on everything under your control every chance you get.

You'll be the life of every party, trust us. Ladies dig OSSTMM guys and guys love hearing about OSSTMM from ladies.

In the OSI model, these are Layer 7 attacks. Since everyone including your grandmother has a web page or uses the Internet, a large number of network attacks are aimed at web applications. Organizations may not use secure coding practices for in-house programs and many lack the resources to perform proper security auditing of their public web application software. This common industry practice leaves more exploits open with every new web widget and web application. Mobile applications are easy targets because more people have smartphones than computers. More people put sensitive information on their smartphones, too. They also take their smartphones to work with them. It's a win-win situation for every attacker.

Low-level application vulnerabilities can be chained together to run a series of commands with the privileges of the "root" user on the device. An attacker can obtain unauthorized access to the device and plant backdoors or access configuration files containing credentials for other systems (like Active Directory/LDAP credentials) that can be used in further attacks.

Then there are the apps practically everyone uses, like Adobe Reader and Flash. Apple refuses to offer Adobe Flash in iOS because they feel Adobe has too many unsolved security issues. And that's just a video plug-in.

Let's take a look at how many applications run on a small device. Even before you turn the device on, there is an internal clock. You turn your device on and the circus starts. As power is applied, it is monitored by an on-board application that checks to ensure correct voltage. If it has enough juice, then the built-in circuits check to see what sort of thing they're in. It might be a toaster, it might be a Titan super computer, it just needs an application to see what its initial purpose is.

Before we have even the slightest evidence of life on the screen, we have already run three to four applications. The device's read-only memory lives in built-in chips that use a hard coded application to tell the OS about its size, file storage capacity, if it's bootable, did it pass the self-test, things like that. We are running five applications and the device isn't even ready to work yet. Yet, each one of the internal applications communicates with each other and the CPU before you see the start screen. Once that device is operational, you could easily have thirty programs running just on your smartphone. Let's multiply that a few hundred times for a desktop computer and multiply that a thousand times more for networks.

Application level attack potential changes every time a new device or program is added, updated, removed or reconfigured.

Updates and patches are the traditional solution to application vulnerabilities. Oops, this form is vulnerable to XSS; better fix it. Dang, that input allows a buffer overflow; better fix that too. Fix that buggy code by piling on thousands of more lines of buggy code! Or fail completely, as some patches do, and crash ALL your users' systems (it's happened more than once).

Some attacks use file replacement to keep their activity hidden. Malware and other attack techniques will name their programs "calc.exe" or "notepad" to hide them in plain sight within the victim's network. As the victim updates their programs, that malicious code can be overwritten with the correct application. To combat this, an attacker will usually place a second copy of their code somewhere else in the system. This second copy will routinely check to make sure the attack package is where it was meant to be. If the malware is overwritten, the second copy just writes it there again.

Exercises

7.16 Mobile devices aren't exempt from malware. List the application marketplaces for the top three mobile operating systems.

7.17 For each marketplace, do research to determine if they have ever distributed malware. If it has, how was it delivered? How did it get into the market? And what type of malware was it?

7.18 What is Project un1c0rn? Go to their website. What are you looking at? How can you use this information?

Remote Access Toolkits (RATs)

This type of attack can be used by the very beginner script kiddie but it is still an effective method to obtain access to networks and data. You don't have to know anything about scripting to launch preconfigured programs like Poison Ivy. They provide remote access that's almost identical to Windows Remote Desktop. Have you used it? It's useful for troubleshooting, training and breaking into a computer from a distance.

Let's say that you forgot a file on your home computer but you are at the coffee shop. Remote Desktop into your home computer and transmit that file to your new location or even work on that file as if you were sitting at the home computer. It's quite handy. It's also quite dangerous if not configured correctly.

That is the key to security for all digital life forms: configure them correctly.

Right out of the box, most products and applications are designed to be used by the widest possible population using the most open configuration settings. This means things are supposed to be easy for the least computer savvy person you know, like a grandparent. It's up to the user to configure, tweak, lock down and most importantly, read the manual. You may have heard the phrase "RTM." (Sometimes people add another initial.) Yup, that stands for "read the manual." Most people don't.

Weak passwords are easy ways to gain access to remote connections. You could stand outside any public hotspot, sniff the packets for a few minutes and you will probably obtain several passwords for company remote servers. We at Hacker Highschool do not recommend that you do this, but this is the kind of testing a smart security person will do, along with warning network users to stay away from public access WiFi unless proper protection measures are taken (hint: a secure VPN).

Exercises

7.19 Who are the primary users of RATs, and for what purpose? This may be a tricky question to answer until you do some research on **Advanced Persistent Threats (APTs)**. (We discussed these in Lesson 6, Malware.) APTs frequently use RATs.

7.20 If you scanned your own computer for open ports, which port number would make you suspect it was infected with a RAT?

DOS and DDOS

Denial of Service (DoS) attacks and **Distributed Denial of Service (DDoS)** attacks are commonly associated with web sites and ecommerce. However, both of these attacks can be used against any device that communicates: an email server, a proxy, a switch, an IDS and so forth. We are just used to hearing of these being used against web servers.

We are experiencing massive demand on our support capacity, we are going to get to everyone it will just take time.

Code Spaces : Is Down!

Dear Customers,

On Tuesday the 17th of June 2014 we received a well orchestrated DDOS against our servers, this happens quite often and we normally overcome them in a way that is transparent to the Code Spaces community. On this occasion however the DDOS was just the start.

An **unauthorised** person who at this point who is still unknown (All we can say is that we have no reason to think its anyone who is or was employed with Code Spaces) had gained access to our Amazon EC2 control panel and had left a number of messages for us to contact them using a hotmail address

Reaching out to the address started a chain of events that revolved arount the person trying to extort a large fee in order to resolve the DDOS.

Upon realisation that somebody had access to our control panel we started to investigate how access had been gained and what access that person had to the data in our systems, it became clear that so far **no** machine access had been achieved due to the intruder not having our Private Keys.

Figure 7.1 *The Codespaces.com DDOS*

Web attacks occur so often that they don't make headlines anymore. One of the major problems with web attacks is the loss of business that happens when a company can't conduct transactions over the web. Amazon, Google, Facebook, the New York Times and every major web content provider has been the target of DoS or DDoS attacks. The basic idea behind these attacks is to keep a web server network too busy to handle normal IP traffic. These attacks can be as simple as sending partial header requests to a server or as complicated as having tens of thousands of zombie computers overload a network with bogus requests.

Due to the limitations of a single computer, it is difficult for one machine to disrupt the service of a communication server. This isn't to say that there are no DoS attacks. There are and we'll show you one in particular. But you're more likely to see large networks of computers working to distribute an attack across multiple fronts to disable networks. This is a DDoS attack. Those are much more common and it's harder to track the true attackers.

DDoS requires a massive network of machines that are infected with command and control software that propagates across thousands of unsuspecting computers. Most of the time, the computer owner has no idea that they are part of a DDoS. These machines are controlled by higher-level control servers located throughout the area. Above the controlled servers is the mothership server that passes commands down to the control servers, which they relay to the individual bots/zombies.

Locating the control servers is difficult at best and finding the mothership is rare. If the control servers are located or compromised, the mothership servers unplug and disappear. In the meantime, the individually controlled computers that unwittingly participated in the DDoS cannot be legally prosecuted since they didn't know they were part of a crime. Right? (Wrong.)

Criminal hackers have figured out many new twists on the DDoS concept but those ideas are beyond the scope of this lesson. We'll be covering a range of DoS and DDoS attacks and how they work.

Exercise

7.21 Read up on Rustock.

- Is it a trojan?

- Is it a root kit?

- Is it a proxy?

- Is it a back door?

- Find out how to remove it. Particularly note the Registry keys and the files you have to remove.

- And once you have, is that really the end of your problems?

Feed Your Head: A DDOS Attack

Distributed Denial of Service (DDoS) attacks are common against ecommerce and just about any organization with a website is open for such attacks. The reasons range from revenge to ransom. Many of these attacks are handled by the victim in a crisis mode with little attention paid to preserving the attack methodology. Here at Hacker

Highschool, we like to see the gory details of these events.

Luckily, there have been a few DDoS events that were either documented, recorded, taped or somehow preserved for our viewing. Here are a few of these attacks and what information was released during the events.

The GitHub attack on 1 October 2013

GitHub is a repository of code for programmers to share. It is sort of like a library of scripts and fully functional programs with a massive collection of users and participants. Over the course of a week, GitHub was hit with several flavors of DDoS. The first phase began with the attacker testing GitHub to see which vulnerabilities would work against the servers.

The initial wave of the attack was fairly unsuccessful so the attacker tweaked their DDoS towards other known vulnerabilities. The second and third phases were able to shut down the GitHub web servers. These days, DDoS attacks have come in waves over the course of a few days. The first part of the attack is actually the recon portion, where the DDoS is looking to see which weaknesses the servers respond to. The initial attack stops for a day while the attacker refines the attack perimeters and sets up the full-fledged DDoS.

Once the perpetrator had a good night's sleep and some breakfast, the aggressor resumes the duties of conducting the massive DDoS. Here are the victim's site postings from the attack. Pay attention to the time stamps on each message. The messages are in reverse order so that's why you need to look at the time and dates of each announcement.

GitHub Status

Updated about 18 hours ago

Status Messages

https://status.github.com/messages

October 02, 2013

12:35 UTC The attack has subsided and services have recovered. We're keeping mitigation in place to ensure we're able to quickly react if the attack returns.

11:31 UTC We've restored access to code downloads and queued service hooks are being delivered. The attack continues, but our mitigation is holding firm.

11:15 UTC Transit connectivity has been restored for some users. We are still actively mitigating a large attack.

10:48 UTC We're working to re-establish connectivity after the attack disrupted our primary Internet transit links.

10:20 UTC The site is unavailable as we continue mitigating a large DDoS attack.

10:17 UTC Service hook delivery is delayed and archived generation unavailable while the attack continues. We're simultaneously working on deflecting the attack and restoring affected services.

9:43 UTC We are recovering from a major service outage as we work to mitigate another DDoS attack.

9:35 UTC The site is unavailable as we investigate issues reaching GitHub.com.

October 01, 2013

22:17 UTC Everything operating normally.

22:07 UTC We are investigating issues with the GitHub API

20:39 UTC The DDoS attack has stopped and service should be back to normal. We're keeping a close eye on things to ensure we're able to quickly mitigate the attack if it returns.

20:23 UTC The site remains available as we continue to mitigate a large and growing DDoS attack. There may be some isolated problems as we apply different mitigation strategies.

20:09 UTC Everything operating normally.

20:01 UTC The site is available again as we work to mitigate the DDoS.

19:59 UTC We are working to mitigate a large scale DDoS attack.

19:58 UTC We are investigating issues reaching all GitHub sites, including git operations.

19:54 UTC We are investigating issues reaching GitHub.com.

The VideoLAN Attack

We all know that a picture is worth a thousand words, but how many words is a video of a DDoS attack worth? HHS is guessing that it is worth pages of words so we've located a video of such an attack that occurred on 23 April 2013. The makers of VideoLAN built a log visualization tool called Logstalgia. It shows traffic entering from the left, being handled by servers on the right (and a paddle from the antique Pong game). Here's what normal traffic looks like:

http://www.youtube.com/watch?v=HeWfkPeDQbY

Using Logstalgia, the developers were able to record most of the attack. If you look on the left side of the screen, you'll see the DDoS packets coming at the servers. The right side of the screen is the VideoLAN servers and their response to the DDoS. The site used a product called Aplomb (which, BTW, is an actual word) to protect themselves against a 400-packets-per-second request attack.

http://www.youtube.com/watch?v=hNjdBSola8k

So, looking at the video you'll see the attack coming in as packet requests from the left side and the attack response battling back from the right side. If you use your imagination, you could almost picture a massive field with Ninjas on one side and M-1 Abrams tanks on the other. Or maybe even a bunch of angry zebras on one side and declawed lions on the other. Hey, it's your imagination, you think of whatever makes you happy.

Here are the Tweets from the attacked servers:

Ludovic Fauvet @etixxx 23 Apr

The attack is still going strong against the VideoLAN infrastructures but still no downtime expected at the moment.

Diego Elio Pettenò @flameeyes 23 Apr

@etixxx how's @ModSecurity performing?

Ludovic Fauvet @etixxx 23 Apr

@flameeyes @ModSecurity Nginx is doing the job. The attack is targeting http://get.videolan.org

:-)

ModSecurity @ModSecurity 23 Apr

@etixxx @flameeyes what type of attack? DoS?

Ludovic Fauvet @etixxx

@ModSecurity @flameeyes DDOS on our download infrastructure yes. But for now they are still using a common user-agent so we're fine.

4:45 AM - 23 Apr 13

Diego Elio Pettenò @flameeyes 23 Apr

@etixxx @ModSecurity remember you can use modsec for nginx as well...

Ludovic Fauvet @etixxx 23 Apr

@flameeyes @ModSecurity Great! I didn't know that.

ModSecurity @ModSecurity 23 Apr

@etixxx @flameeyes http://blog.spiderlabs.com/2012/09/announcing-the-availability-of-modsecurity-extension-for-nginx.html ...

Stuck in the Honeypot

Honeypots have been used for information gathering on cyber activities for years. Some of the larger honeypot projects involved hundreds of servers from various organizations working together to see how crackers work.

One such honeypot project was conducted by Google, where they set up all kinds of traps all over the place in hopes of learning how hackers hack. During one of the events, they spotted a DDoS as it was taking place. Imagine that! Anyway, enough sarcasm. Here is a brief video in very poor quality showing a DDoS as it is playing out.

http://www.youtube.com/watch?v=dl_CUHVUQh0

Hey, don't blame us, we didn't make the video.

Slowdowns

Let's start with the simple slow Denial of Service attack. A program like **Slowloris** sends HTTP header packets to the victim. The trick is that the packets Slowloris sends are never complete requests or they don't contain all the information the web server needs to respond to the HTTP request. Think of it as the old joke, "How do you keep an idiot in suspense? I'll tell you tomorrow."

The attack tries to make as many connections as possible. This is a slow attack, like you getting out of bed on a cold morning. Slowloris mainly works against older Apache servers, where the server will wait for the full header information before processing that request. The attack will send additional HTTP information but never enough to complete the request; it just tries to keep the connection open as long as possible.

This attack can be mitigated by limiting the number of connections a single IP address can open and restricting slow connections to a minimum. Newer Apache server software comes with a module to reduce the effectiveness of this attack called mod_reqtimeout.

Unicorns

UDP Unicorn attacks User Datagram Protocol, which is the primeval portion of the Internet protocols. Remember way back when we talked about protocols? Yeah, we told you about the connectionless UDP that doesn't use any handshakes, unlike TCP (all that SYN – SYN ACK stuff). It just sends data and forgets about it. This works great for streaming video, when data is being sent in large masses and missing one or five packets isn't going to be noticed by the user.

The Unicorn attack exploits **Windows sockets (Winsock)** to make your dreams come true. It does this by flooding a target with multithreaded UDP packets. Similar UDP-LAG attacks just try to slow down a server, thus the name "Lag." It takes a pretty fat connection to overload another server but this is an old school method of attack that is still out there, lagging.

Pay Per Service

Imagine this: you can buy criminal **Software-as-a-Service (SaaS)**. Usually SaaS is something like email services, but there have been, are and will be services like Blackhole where you could pay by the thousand computers for sophisticated attacks against the victim of your choice. Of course, this service business earned its creator, Paunch, many exciting adventures with the Russian legal and prison systems. Another pay-to-hack too is TwBooter, a web service that calls itself an "Administrative Network Stresser Tool." Whatever you want to call it, it does things similar to Blackhole. You give it a target, pay your fee and clap your hands in glory as you watch some web site become the victim of a DoS. No intelligence required.

Getting to Post

GET and POST attacks overwhelm a victim's server by filling up their memory buffers with requests. Some of the attacks require the server to decrypt its own data in a circular process. It's kind of like that annoying game where you repeat everything the other person says. In this attack, though, the server has no idea it is repeating itself thousands of times a minute.

HTTP GET Flooding is exactly what its name says: it floods the victim with GET requests to overwhelm the network. The GET and POST attacks work very well in SSL sessions under HTTPS. These attacks are more difficult to identify because the data requests are encrypted.

RUDY, or the **R-U-Dead-Yet** attack, is a form of POST attack, but it works by sending a never-ending content length request for a POST query. The server keeps waiting for the rest of the POST content length but it never comes. It's like winning the lottery: It never happens, to you anyway.

DDoS By the Numbers

Distributed Denial of Service attacks require lots of data and plenty of bandwidth to overwhelm the victim's servers. To achieve this feat, most attackers will leverage other resources like botnets, using other servers (that don't belong to them), or being really creative with protocols. DDoS attacks utilize almost every layer of the OSI model (remember the OSI model from earlier lessons?) and the protocols associated with them.

Layer 3 and 4 attacks have used the Network Time Protocol (NTP) servers to flood targets with amplified data requests. The protocol was designed back when the Internet was young and security wasn't an issue. Many of the original internet protocols are still used today and still lack basic security measures. With the NTP attack, an attacker spoofs a request for time from one of the NTP servers located throughout the world to synchronize time across networks. A NTP request is a small unauthenticated request from one computer for a time update. The NTP returns to the requestor a longer string of data that includes the time.

In this attack, the data requested is amplified by the fact the NTP server returns more data than is sent to it in the first place. The NTP servers don't require verification from the requesting user which allows an attacker to spoof the return IP address. An attacker sets up crafted packets that have the target as the destination address. These packets can be launched from a single server that allows IP spoofing.

One attack on 10 February 2014 generated a peak of 400 Gbps against a cloud server. Now that is some serious amplification of data directed at a target. The requests generate 206 times more data than are sent. So if the attacker sends 1,000 8 bit NTP requests (MONLIST) at 1,000 NTP servers, the results will be 16,480,000 bits sent back to a target. It's slightly more technical than this but you get the idea.

Switches in protocols and commands are being leveraged to create massive floods of data against targets. The Open DNS attack works the same way but doesn't return as much data as the NTP attack. A similar attack using SNMP servers could yield a return of data at 650 times the rate.

Exercises

7.22 You want to launch an attack against the computer of someone in your class, and you're interested in Low Orbit Ion Cannon (LOIC).

- Will it do what you want?

- Can you find it online? Do so.

- How do you use it? Explain.

7.23 Find information on attack trees. Create an attack tree that diagrams the steps necessary for you to launch a LOIC attack against your classmate's computer.

Malware (Nobody liked me as a kid)

If you haven't read the lesson yet, don't forget that Lesson 6 deals with malware.

In the early days of viruses, many would simply delete the victim's data. Others would play a silly tune while wiping the file allocation table or posting a message announcing to the user that the computer is infected. These were very destructive programs and only seemed to come in a few flavors.

Those flavors were:

1. Delete data on the computer.

2. Overload networks by propagation and resource hogging.

3. Just plain messing with users' heads by deleting text, changing page order, altering typed characters and so on. The kind of stuff your kid brother does to you, or you do to your big sister.

These early forms of malware evolved into polymorphic (able to change their own structure to avoid signature detection), macro level scripts (which depended on a particular application like MS Word) and somewhat more sophisticated programs that began extorting money from users. Virus makers turned to profitable **ransomware** programs that encrypt user data and demand money from the computer owner to decrypt the data. As you might expect, those that paid the ransom did not always get their data back. (Surprise: Pirate.)

Malware began its life as a form of attacking computers and that fact hasn't changed one byte.

Teaching a man to phish (Hacking the Wetware)

Delivering these malware packages to someone's system has become much easier. Phishing is the primary method, although did you check out that USB drive you found lying in the driveway? Great new program on it wasn't there? We spent the whole night reworking it so that when you put in into your computer it loaded our software along with the game. When you are done playing with the game and your computer, we will launch our attacks, using your system, your IP and your persona. If you want to see how much you know about phishing, the OpenDNS quiz is a good place to start (http://www.opendns.com/phishing-quiz/).

Exercises

7.24 Put your security consultant hat on again. Your client wants to know if security training really is effective in making employees safer. There are big names on both sides of the debate.

- List two Godzilla-class security professionals who say it isn't effective, and very briefly, why.

- List two who say it is, and why.

7.25 Now you selling your client on SET (the Social-Engineer Toolkit). What the heck does it do? Are you selling him a product, or services?

Hacking the Technology that Surrounds Us

One of the hottest topics in the technology world is the **Internet of Things (IoT)**, the networked devices that include everything from your home's electric meter to the **tire pressure management system (TPMS)** on the cars around you. Most of these communicate using familiar protocols, which means most of them can be manipulated using familiar methods: spoofing, DDoS, physical mischief, etc.

Exercises

7.26 What is the wireless protocol used by TPMSs?

- How does your car know which sensors are its own, when every car around it has them too?

- Is this identification method susceptible to spoofing? DDoS? What else? In other words, are there vulnerabilities in this system?

7.27 Does the car you're in most often have a built-in GPS unit?

- What are the vulnerabilities in THIS system?

Attack Signatures: Detecting Different Types of Attacks

Some attacks are like mosquito bites: you don't notice them until after you've been bitten (and had all your blood sucked out). Other attacks can take place over months and years, siphoning off your proprietary data the entire time.

A spoofing attack can remain hidden inside a network while a DDoS will wake up the entire IT staff as the phone begin ringing off the hook. Everyone will be asking, why did you take the network down? You didn't. You were eating a sandwich. Somebody else is taking your network down.

Attack detection techniques rely on **signature recognition** and **anomaly detection**. Signature detection works great if the attacker is using known vulnerabilities, exploits, or typical tools (like script kiddies do). The problem with looking for attack signatures is that the programs need to know what those are ahead of time. Signature recognition programs don't work against zero-day exploits because there isn't any signature to detect until after the attack.

Anomalies within a network are an everyday occurrence. If the intrusion detection system sends an alarm every time a data burst occurs, you'll be spending your entire work day resetting the system. A few bad log-on attempts and there goes your weekend. From a practical standpoint: what is an anomaly anyway? There is no easy method to distinguish normal data flow from an attack, other than a DDoS or DoS. And deep packet inspections require additional resources and possible delays in data transmission.

Network attacks that are carried out by people unfamiliar with your company will gather information ahead of time. Scanning by outside IP addresses is a normal part of any network so you will have to look for certain patterns like:

1. Scans that repeat the same time each day or night (weekends and holidays are great times to recon networks)

2. Scans that come from within the domain (because internal scans are considered "passive" traffic, the attacker may not bother with a disguise)

3. Scans that seem to use the same technique/tool

4. Scans that seem to come from an internal IP address

5. Scans that focus on known or new vulnerabilities (CVEs)

6. Scans against hardware such as routers, IDS, printers and other network connected devices. They all have IP addresses so they make great access points.

7. WiFi network scans, Bluetooth scans and remote access log-in attempts from portable devices in the local area. Look at that coffee shop across the street.

Exercise

7.28 Here's where you begin your education with the open-source intrusion-detection application, Snort. First, find the website where Snort is distributed and supported.

7.29 Like many malware detectors, Snort relies heavily on signatures. Find a Snort signature for the CryptoLocker malware.

The Spoof

Spoofing may be detectable by tracking redirected URLs in user web browsers (or by disallowing redirects altogether). Spotting spoofed sites in email links is fairly tough because of the social engineering factor: People are curious and trusting. Training and educating company staff is a good starting point for preventing users from clicking on malware-linked sites. The problem is hackers are excellent at enticing a user to open up or click on a things. You know what you do when you get an email from your mother that tells you to look at some video of your relative doing something funny. One click and the payload is already loaded. Too bad, no video of Uncle Mika slipping in the bathroom.

Spoofing may be used as part of an overall complex attack, such as reconnaissance or information gathering. Creating a spoofed web site might be a simple method to get network users to upload a small segment of a larger attack tool. It would be like getting one foot in a network's door. Once that small script or program is inside a user's browsers, the malware phones home to retrieve the rest of the program. These actions can be detected if you are looking for outbound traffic on unexpected ports to unusual URLs. You should not see a local user uploading data to an external source; this is almost always a bad thing. Too few network security professionals look at outbound activities, though, for better or worse, depending on which side you're on.

IP packet spoof detection requires more work since only a few of the current network protocols confirm the authenticity of inbound data packet addresses. Forged certificates, man-in-the-middle intercepts and hijacked sessions can all be made to look like trusted data sources. Add to the fact that spoofing can happen at multiple network levels such as network layer spoofing, transport layer spoofing, session and application layer spoofing (discussed earlier) and data link layer (MAC address) spoofing.

Proper identification of suspected spoofed data packets needs to work in conjunction with IDS, routers and firewalls within a network. An intruder may not even use the reply data that your network provided, they may just be looking for a connection. If she asks for DNS resolution from inside your network, she may not care if she gets a correct DNS entry back (although this could be handy); she's just probing for hosts. Usually. This is where **Time to Live (TTL)** becomes useful for not only detecting spoofed packets but stopping spoofed data. Basically, the TTL setting of a packet tells the network how long to keep kicking the packet around. Packets shouldn't be hanging around forever, and if they are trying to, they deserve suspicion.

Inside intranets, data packets traveling along similar routes should take roughly the same path and arrive at the same time, every time. If there are packets that do not seem to follow this basic principle, or appear to bounce through different paths, those packets may be spoofed. Routers automatically tune TTLs (keep them as short as possible) to minimize and flush out wandering (spoofed) packets. This is a basic first line of defense.

However, different protocols use different TTLs. This is one reason why you will need to depend on correctly configured firewalls, routers and user training. Spoofing is a constant challenge to battle.

Exercises

7.30 Time for research: find one common command-line tool that lets you find the path to a target, using a switch that specifies the maximum number of hops (TTL), as a way to detect spoofing. (Yes, you have used this tool before, in earlier lessons.)

7.31 And more research: find one easily-available command-line tool that lets you create spoofed packets (or heck, any kind of packets you can imagine).

Sniffles

Sniffing packets is not as simple as plugging your computer into the network and capturing traffic. It's often more difficult to decide where to place the sniffer than it is to analyze the traffic. The main devices that handle network traffic do so differently, so you have to be aware of the network's physical setup. So, how do you collect traffic from the network?

First, if you're going to have to collect *everyone's* traffic, on a wired Ethernet network you'll need a **mirror port** or **trunk port** on a switch. Otherwise, on a switched network, the only traffic you'll see is broadcast traffic and your own. But be very clear: WiFi is not switched networking. WiFi functions like a hub: you can see everyone's packets.

If you're attached to a mirror port or have put your WiFi card into **promiscuous mode**, a packet sniffer application can monitor network traffic on all computers on the network.

Packet Sniffing

A packet sniffing program is designed to capture the traffic packets that move along the network. You get to check out the packet content and make some determinations about the validity of the packet. In Linux/Mac/Unix, the native **tcpdump** command can capture traffic, save it to a file, look for search strings and a lot more. When you're dealing with automated processes (come on, you're a hacker, you want to automate everything), using tcpdump at the command line is the way to go.

Enter the Shark: Wireshark

Full-on GUI tools like **Wireshark** are often called **network protocol analyzers**. They let you capture and interactively browse the traffic running on a computer network. Wireshark is the de facto (and often **de jure** [by law]) standard across many industries and educational institutions. For Windows users, you must also install the **WinPcap** driver, which you'll be reminded of during installation. WinPcap is also available from www.winpacap.polito.it, if you find yourself needing it separately.

Windows Installation

Download and install Wireshark (http://www.wireshark.org). Then follow these steps:

1. Double-click the installer file to begin installation and then click **Next** in the introductory window.

2. Accept defaults all the way through.

3. **When the dialog asks if you want to install WinPcap, make sure the Install WinPcap box is checked (indicating "yes").**

4. Click **Install** and the process will begin.

Linux Install

The first step to installing Wireshark on Linux is to download the correct installation package. Not all versions are supported. Usually you're going to need root privileges.

RPM-based Systems

For RPM-based distributions (Red Hat, Fedora and SUSE), you can download the appropriate package from the Wireshark page. Open a terminal window and a command like this (use the filename of the actual installation package you download):

    rpm –ivh wireshark-0.99.3.i386.rpm

But you can usually install it without downloading it with this command:

    yum install wireshark

This command goes out and gets a slick pre-configured package from the **system repositories** and installs it for you. Nice, huh?

DEB-based Systems

On a DEB-based system (Debian, Ubuntu and many more) you can install Wireshark from system repositories, so you don't need to download anything unless you really want to here either. Open a terminal window and type the following:

    apt-get install wireshark

Mac OS X Install

Different versions of Mac OS X require different procedures to install Wireshark. Check the online documentation, but generally the steps are:

1. Download the DMG package from the Wireshark site, and the Xquartz package from http://xquartz.macosforge.org.

2. Open the Wireshark.dmg and copy Wireshark.app to the Applications folder.

3. Open the Xquartz.dmg and copy Xquarz to the Applications/Utilities folder.

4. When you start Wireshark you'll be prompted to *Choose Application for X11* since it doesn't find it up in the Applications folder. You need to manually locate it by browsing down to it in Applications/Utilities/XQuartz.

Wireshark Fundamentals

To find anomalies on your network when you might be under attack, you'll have to know what daily normal network activity looks like. With your network operating smoothly, you can baseline your activities. Deviations from this baseline mean something is amiss.

Exercise

7.32 Packet capture with Wireshark: follow these steps.

Open Wireshark, and from the main drop-down menu, select **Capture** and then **Interface**. A list of interfaces with their IP address should be visible.

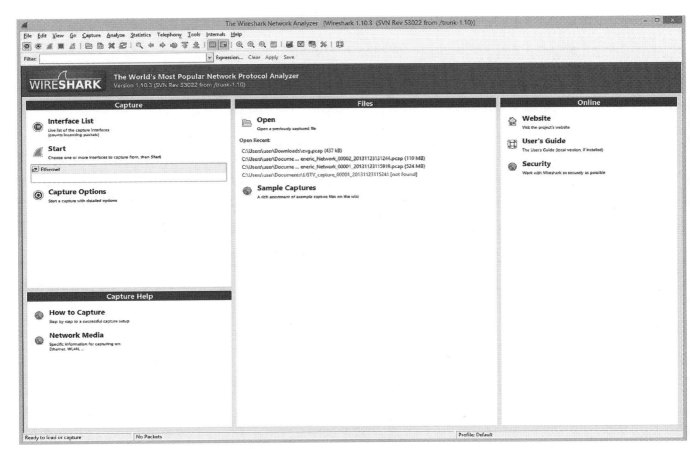

Figure 7.1 *Wireshark*

Choose the interface you want to use and click **Start** or simply click the interface under the Interface List section. Data should start filling the window.

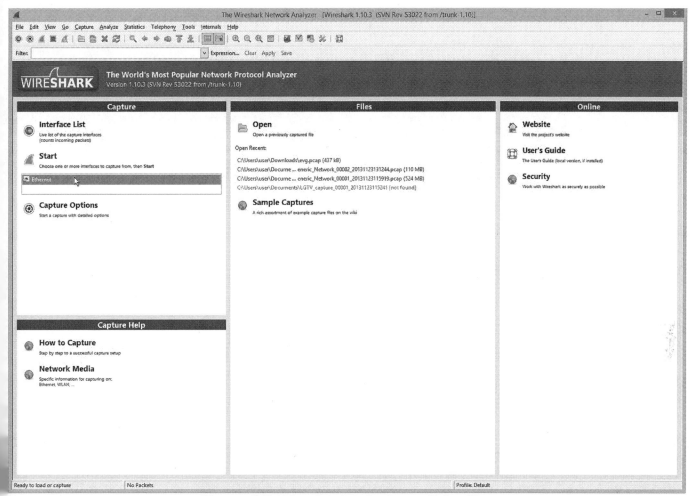

Figure 7.2 *Wireshark Interface Selection*

This will open another window that shows the activity that Wireshark sees on your network.

Open each of the following screens in your local copy of Wireshark.

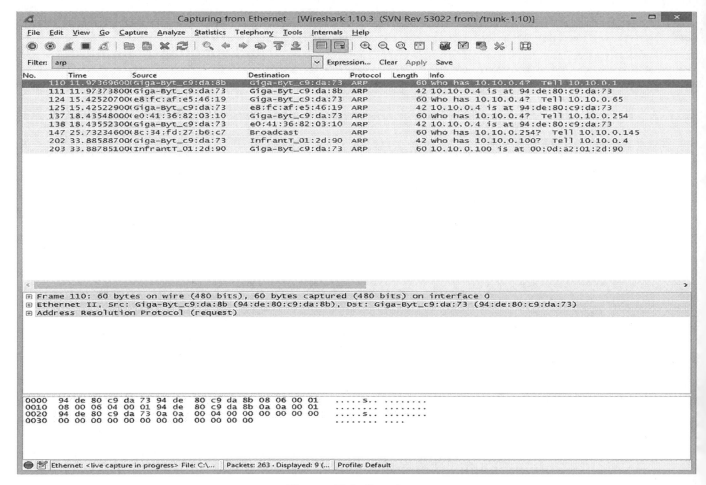

Figure 7.3 *Capture*

In the packet capture window, the top pane displays a table containing all the packets in the current capture file. This includes the packet number, the relative time of the packet capture, the source and destination of the packet, the packet's protocol and some general information found in the packet.

The middle pane contains a hierarchical display of the information about a single packet.

The lower pane displays the packet in its raw, unprocessed form. It shows how the packet looked as it crossed the wire.

Decoding the Packets

Now that you can see network traffic, you have to figure out what it all means. Wireshark provides a number of charts that are valuable in establishing what normal network traffic looks like. There are a lot of different statistics to consult: click on the *Statistics* field in the menu bar at the top of the screen.

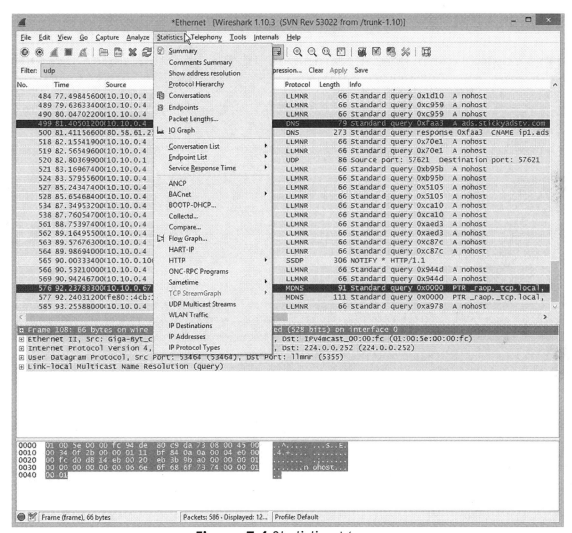

Figure 7.4 *Statistics Menu*

These statistics are compilations of data Wireshark observed. Conversations and endpoints identify sources of significant amounts of traffic. This tells you what the traffic flow of your network should look like. Some items you might consider looking at include ARP or ICMP packets. Large numbers of such packets might suggest a problem.

Wireshark Summary Screen

Basic global statistics are available in the summary window such as:

- Capture file properties

- Capture time

- Capture filter information

- Display filter information

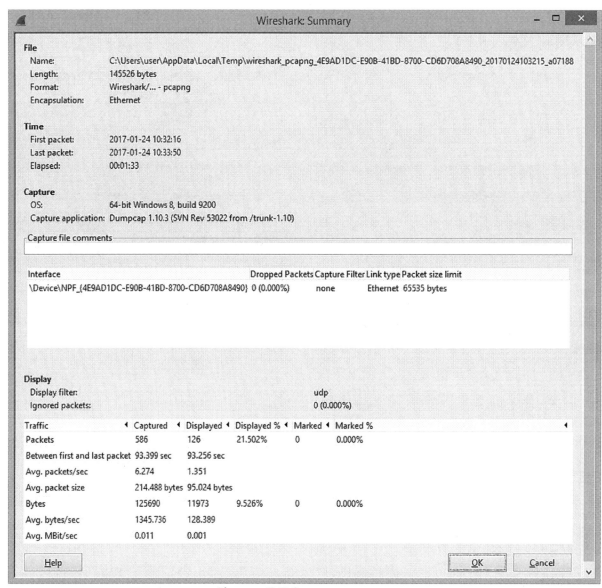

Figure 7.5 *Summary*

Protocol Hierarchy

The protocol hierarchy shows a dissection by OSI layer of the displayed data.

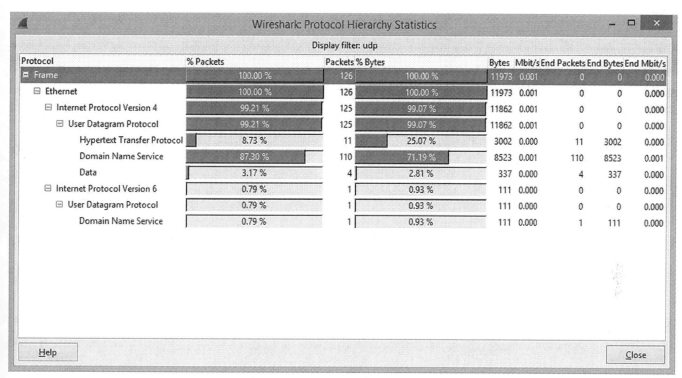

Figure 7.6 *Protocol Hierarchy*

Conversations

If you use a TCP/IP application or protocol, you should find four active tabs for Ethernet, IP, TCP and UDP conversations. A "conversation" represents the traffic between two hosts. The number in the tab after the protocol indicates the number of conversations, for example "Ethernet:6".

Ethernet Conversations

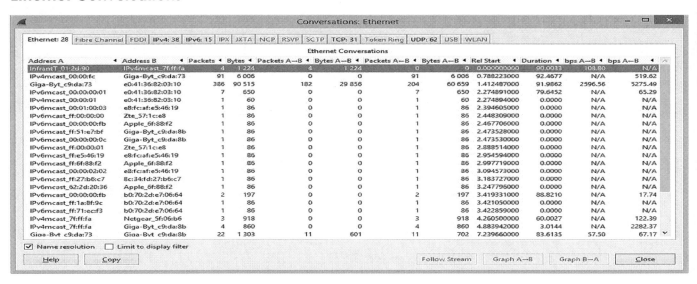

Figure 7.7 *Ethernet Conversations*

IP Conversations

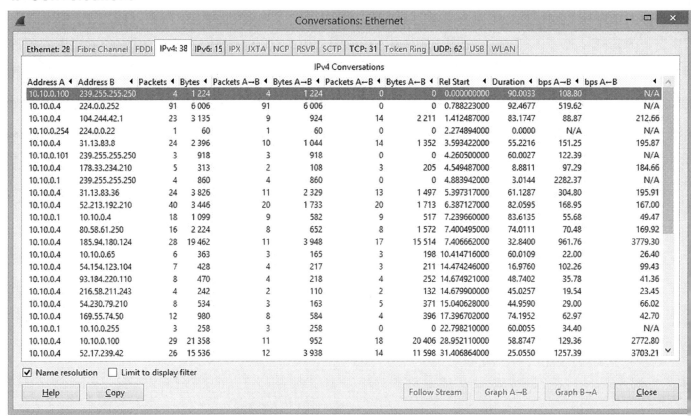

Figure 7.8 *IP Conversations*

TCP Conversations

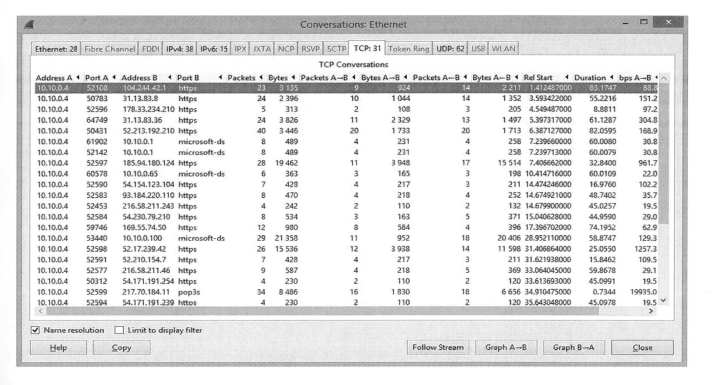

Figure 7.9 *TCP Conversations*

As you review this information from your computer, which programs might be involved in these conversations, in light of information from the lesson on Ports and Protocols?

Endpoints

The endpoints provide statistics about received and transmitted data on a *per machine basis*. The number after the protocol indicates the number of endpoints. For instance: "Ethernet:6".

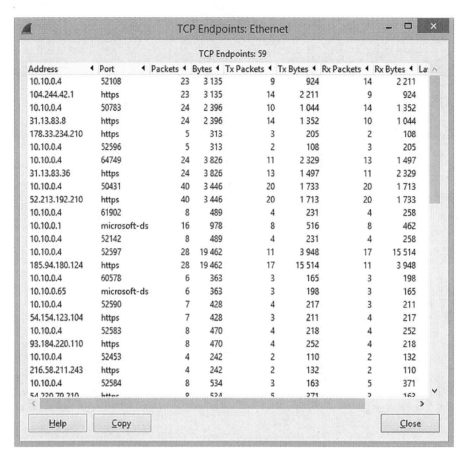

Figure 7.10 Endpoints

Output

No.	Time	Source	Destination	Protocol	Length	Info
1	0.000000000	10.10.0.101	239.255.255.250	SSDP	306	NOTIFY * HTTP/1.1
2	0.578147000	10.10.0.1	239.255.255.250	SSDP	215	M-SEARCH * HTTP/1.1
3	0.592415000	10.10.0.4	224.0.0.252	LLMNR	66	Standard query 0xacdc A nohost
4	1.003698000	10.10.0.4	224.0.0.252	LLMNR	66	Standard query 0xacdc A nohost
5	1.062668000	10.10.0.4	169.55.74.50	TLSv1.2	92	Application Data
6	1.147664000	10.10.0.4	31.13.83.36	SSL	55	Continuation Data
7	1.161615000	31.13.83.36	10.10.0.4	TCP	60	https > 64749 [ACK] Seq=1 Ack=2 Win=2043 Len=0
8	1.209202000	169.55.74.50	10.10.0.4	TLSv1.2	99	Application Data
9	1.259103000	10.10.0.4	169.55.74.50	TCP	54	59746 > https [ACK] Seq=39 Ack=46 Win=861 Len=0
10	1.345945000	10.10.0.4	80.58.61.250	DNS	80	Standard query 0x49ac A hackerhighschool.org
11	1.372517000	10.10.0.4	80.58.61.254	DNS	80	Standard query 0x49ac A hackerhighschool.org
12	1.578769000	10.10.0.1	239.255.255.250	SSDP	215	M-SEARCH * HTTP/1.1
13	1.599764000	80.58.61.250	10.10.0.4	DNS	146	Standard query response 0x49ac A 216.92.116.13
14	1.600361000	10.10.0.4	216.92.116.13	TCP	66	52758 > http [SYN] Seq=0 Win=8192 Len=0 MSS=1460
15	1.600687000	10.10.0.4	80.58.61.250	DNS	80	Standard query 0x8e51 A hackerhighschool.org
16	1.607039000	10.10.0.4	224.0.0.252	LLMNR	66	Standard query 0xa745 A nohost
17	1.625152000	10.10.0.4	80.58.61.254	DNS	80	Standard query 0x8e51 A hackerhighschool.org

Figure 7.11 Output

In this example, the seventeen packets show activity collected by Wireshark. The easiest information to decode is the *Source* and *Destination* columns. The 10.10.0.X IPs are local network systems. The 169.55.74.50 is not local.

The next column to look at is the *Protocol* column. This column tells you what protocol was being used.

Packets 10, 11, 13, 15, and 17 represent a DNS query to identify a specific website.

The last column, *Info*, provides more detailed information about the packets.

Packets seven and 14 are from the end and subsequent start of two different TCP handshakes:

> Packet 7 – ACK Packet

> Packet 14 – SYN

But there's many other types of packets there like SSDP, LLMNR, TLSv1.2 with Application Data. Look up what these other protocols are and try to understand what Wireshark is seeing there and why. What is traveling over this network?

Exercises

7.33 By now you should be familiar with Wireshark.

- Can you look for a particular string of text in the packets you capture? Find out how.

- Now, start a capture.

- Go to a search engine, and search for the word "password."

- Check in Wireshark: does it see the word "password," or is your traffic encrypted and unreadable?

- Try this with at least three search engines.

- Which ones encrypt your traffic? Why do you suppose they do this?

- Be clear that this is exactly how information is leaked: when it's outbound.

7.34 Are you getting tired of looking at individual packets? Now it's time to learn about a nice feature of Wireshark called "following TCP streams." The whole idea of TCP is taking traffic apart and putting it back together again, so why not get rid of the whole "packetizing" operation and look at the original data?

7.35 You are a double-top-secret agent, and you've managed to break into the Elbownian Embassy's VoIP system. You are familiar with Voice over IP, right? Basically it's telephone over the Internet. Use Wireshark to see how many VoIP calls are active.

7.36 If you can pinpoint the TCP stream for a VoIP call, and you can follow that stream, and you can save that stream, can you play back that call?

Hubs, Routers and Switches

The functions of a router, hub and a switch are all quite different even if at times they are all integrated into a single device. Let's start with the hub and the switch since these two devices have similar roles on the network. Each serves as a central connection for all of your network equipment and handles a data type known as **ethernet frames**. Frames carry your data. When a frame is received, it is transmitted on to the physical port the destination PC is plugged into. The big difference between these two devices is in the method for delivering frames.

In a **hub**, incoming frames are broadcasted to all ports. It doesn't matter that the frame is only destined for one machine. The hub has no way of distinguishing which port a frame should be sent to. Passing it along to every port ensures that it will reach its intended destination. This puts a lot of traffic on the network and can lead to poor network response times. Since a hub broadcasts every packet to every machine or node on the hub, a filter in each computer discards packets not addressed to it. A packet sniffer disables this filter to capture and analyze some or all packets traveling through the hub, depending on the sniffer's configuration.

A **switch**, on the other hand, keeps a record of the Media Access Control (MAC) or physical addresses of all the devices connected to it. With this information, a switch can identify which system is on which port. So when a frame is received, the switch knows exactly which port to send it to, without significantly increasing network response times. That's why a switch is considered to be a much better choice than a hub. Rather than a central hub that broadcasts all traffic on the network to all machines, the switch acts like a central switchboard. It receives packets directly from the originating computer and sends them directly to the machine to which they are addressed. This makes sniffing packets on a switch much more difficult. You can only see traffic that is intended for your machine - unless you use more advanced techniques such as ARP poisoning (see Ettercap above or Cain and Abel for a Windows tool) By the way, have you noticed that *all* popular sniffing/MITM tools have been developed by Italians? Including the Winpcap port. What's up with that?

Routers are completely different devices. Where a hub or switch is concerned with transmitting ethernet frames at the local Layer 2, a router's job, as its name implies, is to route IP packets to other networks, which is a Layer 3 operation. A packet contains the source address it came from and the data, and the destination address of where it's going.

A router is designed to join two or more networks, commonly two Local Area Networks (LANs) or Wide Area Networks (WANs), or a LAN and its ISP's network. Routers are located at gateways, the places where two or more networks connect. Using headers and forwarding tables, routers determine the best path for forwarding the packets. Routers use protocols like ICMP to communicate with each other and configure the best route between any two hosts. The same packet sniffing issues apply to routers that apply to switches.

Intrusion Detection Systems

You've probably realized that, to use a packet sniffer to detect unauthorized activity in real time, you'll have to sit at your computer, watching the output of the packet sniffer and desperately hoping to see some kind of pattern. An **intrusion detection system (IDS)** does this job for you. IDSs combine the ability to record network activity with sets of rules that allow them to flag unauthorized activity and generate real-time warnings.

Exercises

7.37 Open Wireshark and start a live capture. Now open your web browser and look for a plain text document to download. Download and save the text file to your hard drive, then close the web browser and end the capture session in Wireshark. Look through the packets captured by Wireshark, paying close attention to the ASCII dump in the bottom pane. What do you see? If you have access to an email account, try checking your email while Wireshark is performing a capture. What do you see there?

7.38 On the *Capture Options* Screen, make sure that the box marked "Capture packets in promiscuous mode" is checked. This option may allow you to capture packets directed to or coming from other computers. Begin the capture and see what happens. Do you see any traffic that is intended for a computer other than yours?

7.39 What do you know about the hardware that connects your computer to the network? Does it connect to the other computers through a switch, a router or a hub? Go to a web search engine and try to find out which piece or pieces of hardware would make it most difficult to capture packets from other computers.

7.40 If you are sitting at a coffee shop, library or airport, using WiFi, and you wanted to capture traffic, could you? Could someone else be doing the same to you? What security controls could you use to prevent that?

7.41 Research intrusion detection systems. How are they different from firewalls? What do they have in common with packet sniffers? What kinds of unauthorized activity can they detect? What kinds of activity might they be unable to detect?

Honeypots and Honeynets

People who like to watch monkeys go to the zoo, because there might be monkeys there. People who like to watch birds put out bird feeders and the birds come to them. People who like to watch fish build aquariums and bring the fish to themselves. But what do you do if you want to watch hackers? You put out a **honeypot**. Think about it this way – you're a bear. You may not know much (being a bear) but you do know that honey is tasty and there is nothing better on a warm summer day than a big handful of honey. So you see a big pot full of honey sitting out in the center of a clearing and you're thinking, 'Yum!" But once you stick your paw in the honey pot, you risk getting stuck. If nothing else, you're going to leave big, sticky paw prints everywhere and everyone is going to know that someone has been in the honey and there's a good chance that anyone who follows the big, sticky paw prints is going to discover that it's you. More than one bear has been trapped because he liked tasty honey.

A honeypot is a computer system or virtual machine that serves no other purpose than to lure in hackers. A **honeynet** is a network of honeypots. In a honeypot, there are no authorized users – no real data is stored in the system, no real work is performed on it – so, every access, every attempt to use it, can be identified as unauthorized. Instead of sifting through logs to identify intrusions, the system administrator knows that every access is an intrusion, so a large part of the work is already done.

Types of Honeypots

There are two types of honeypots: production and research.

Production honeypots are used primarily as warning systems. A production honeypot identifies an intrusion and generates an alarm. They can show you that an intruder has identified the system or network as an object of interest, but not much else. For example, if you wanted to know if bears lived near your clearing, you might set out ten tiny pots of honey. If you checked them in the morning and found one or more of them empty, then you would know that bears had been in the vicinity, but you wouldn't know anything else about the bears.

Research honeypots are used to collect information about hacker's activities. A research honeypot lures in hackers and then keeps them occupied while it quietly records their actions. For example, if – instead of simply documenting their presence – you wanted to study the bears then you might set out one big, tasty, sticky pot of honey in the middle of your clearing, but then you would surround that pot with movie cameras, still cameras, tape recorders and research assistants with clipboards and pith helmets.

The two types of honeypots differ primarily in their complexity. You can more easily set up and maintain a production honeypot because of its simplicity and the limited amount of information that you hope to collect. In a production honeypot, you just want to know that you've been hit; you don't care so much whether the hackers stay around. However, in a research honeypot, you want the hackers to stay, so that you can see what they are doing. This makes setting up and maintaining a research honeypot more difficult. You must make the system look like a real, working system that offers files or services that the hackers find interesting. A bear who knows what a honeypot looks like might spend a minute looking at an empty pot, but only a full pot full of tasty honey is going to keep the bear hanging around long enough for you to study it.

Honeynets are harder yet; they have to have what appears to be real, live traffic on them.

Building a Honeypot

In the most basic sense, a honeypot is nothing more than a computer system that is set up with the expectation that it will be compromised by intruders. Essentially, this means that if you connect a computer with an insecure operating system to the Internet, then let it sit there, waiting to be compromised, you have created a honeypot! But this isn't a very useful honeypot. It's more like leaving your honey out in the clearing, then going home to the city. When you come back, the honey will be gone, but you won't know anything about who, how, when or why. You don't learn anything from your honeypot, unless you have some way of gathering information regarding it. To be useful, even the most basic honeypot must have some type of intrusion detection system.

The intrusion detection system could be as simple as a firewall. Normally a firewall is used to prevent unauthorized users from accessing a computer system, but they also log everything that passes through or is stopped. Reviewing the logs produced by the firewall can provide basic information about attempts to access the honeypot.

More complex honeypots might add hardware, such as switches, routers or hubs to further monitor or control network access. They may also use packet sniffers to gather additional information about network traffic.

Research honeypots may also run programs that simulate normal use, making it appear that the honeypot is actually being accessed by authorized users and teasing potential intruders with falsified emails, passwords and data. These types of programs can also be used to disguise operating systems, making it appear, for example, that a Linux based computer is running Windows.

But the thing about honey – it's sticky and there's always a chance that your honeypot is going to turn into a bees' nest. And when the bees come home, you don't want to be the one with your hand stuck in the honey. An improperly configured honeypot can easily be turned into a launching pad for additional attacks. If a hacker compromises your honeypot, then promptly launches an assault on a large corporation or uses your honeypot to distribute a flood of spam, there's a good chance that *you* will be identified as the one responsible.

Correctly configured honeypots control network traffic going into and out of the computer. A simple production honeypot might allow incoming traffic through the firewall, but stop all outgoing traffic. This is a simple, effective solution, but intruders will quickly realize that it is not a real, working computer system. A slightly more complex honeypot might allow some outgoing traffic, but not all.

Research honeypots – which want to keep the intruders interested as long as possible – sometimes use **manglers**, which audit outgoing traffic and disarm potentially dangerous data by modifying it so that it is ineffective.

www.sicherheitstacho.eu has set up live feeds of cyber attacks as they happen. The data is based off 180 sensors (honeypots) located around the world. The site shows who is attacking who, the amount of data in the attack (DDoS), and is updated every few seconds.

Exercises

7.42 Honeypots can be useful tools for research and for spotting intruders, but using them to capture and prosecute these intruders is another question. Different jurisdictions have different definitions and standards and judges and juries often have varying views, so there are many questions that need to be considered. Do honeypots represent an attempt at entrapment in your country?

7.43 Is recording a hacker's activities a form of wiretapping in your country?

7.44 And on the specific question of honeypots – can it be illegal to compromise a system that was designed to be compromised? These questions have yet to be thoroughly tested. Discuss this for a bit – what are your thoughts and why?

Conclusion to Attack Analysis

The news is filled with stories on cyber attacks. Some of the attacks seem sophisticated while others seem to happen by chance. The largest and smallest organizations are being targeted on a regular basis by one form of digital crime or another. Most movie plots involving action have at least one hacker in them that uses Nmap to destroy the enemy. It's like the world has become one big series of digital wars. Expect to see some TV reality show where cyber criminals face off next. Like the next season of *24*.

The reasons for entities to attack each other is as varied as the tools they use. These days most of the attacks are well funded and aimed at criminal behavior. In the old days, attacks were not. Digital crime pays, as does espionage and nation/state warfare. Criminals are using multiple layers of attack to confuse the target.

Financial sectors are being targeted for many types of cyber attacks since that is where the money is. The fastest growing sector for cyber crime is mobile platforms. Malware plays a huge part in the increase of these crimes across the globe. It seems as though attackers are going after anything these days.

To combat and protect yourself, you need to secure your computer/network by thinking about all possible access points. One of the best ways to do this is to think like an attacker. Use the same tools they use against your own domain to see what needs to be strengthened.

Don't focus on the threats as much as your own system. Educate yourself and stay up on news about different types of attacks. The best defense is a good offense. Hacker Highschool encourages you to explore the world around you but do no harm. If you have an issue or a cause, we understand, but caution you to remember the implications of your actions.

Counter Forensics

Introduction to Counter Forensics

If you are attempting to go through all the effort of learning to hack and actually conducting some hacking, you will need to learn how to cover your tracks. It is safe to assume that you will be the focus of an investigation if you pull off a really great hack. Never mind the "whys" and "hows" of the hack; investigators are going to look for evidence to connect you (the suspect) to the crime. The investigators you are interested in are given the lovely name of "Digital Forensic Examiners." That name sounds a bit scary. Don't worry, this lesson will tell you all about those investigators.

Each of the lessons in Hacker Highschool is like a sip of water from a vast ocean of information. You are getting a small taste of the massive topics to whet your appetite for hacking. In this particular lesson, you are being armed with sophisticated knowledge to keep you safe. Knowing how to use this knowledge is entirely up to you. This lesson is going to show you safe locations to put data and how to hide your treasures from prying eyes. What good is hacking a system and obtaining vital information unless you can store your prize in a safe place?

After being a hacker for a while, you will find yourself overloaded with all sorts of media that you need to get rid of. Maybe you don't want that 256 megabyte USB thumb drive anymore. Perhaps that 1 gig SD card is too small for any useful purpose other than a book place marker. Whatever the case might be, it is not a good idea to toss that media in the trash. That old hard drive, yeah, the one you used when you were saving images from lingerie department store web pages. Yes, that drive definitely can't go in the trash in its current condition. We'll show you ways to blow useless data into bits (pun). You'll learn how to ensure nobody ever reads that media again. Evidence needs to be erased.

Once we delete your unwanted collection, you will probably go right back to exploring domains. Hacking a system means that you will leave little clues of your entry, your exploits, and your exit. If these digital tracks are left in the system, you will be getting some attention from the local authorities. You don't want that, do you? Much like your dirty room, you need to know how to clean up after yourself. Everything from concealing your location, altering your entrance methods, changing the system logs time, moving the data without being noticed, and setting up a backdoor needs to be planned for and handled as you go. We'll discuss the best techniques to use.

If you happened to get that dreaded knock on your front door by a team of gun-toting law agents and find yourself on the wrong end of that barrel, we will talk about simple bu effective ways to side step or slow down your investigation. Maybe you need a lawyer, maybe you don't. There are lots of ways to stay one step ahead of law enforcement. There are even more ways to have fun with forensic examiners.

Counter forensics is exactly what the name says it is. Think of digital forensics as a game of hide and go seek; you make all of your moves before the other person even starts. How you apply counter forensic tactics depends on what you are trying to accomplish. Are trying to delete evidence, slow an investigator down, tamper with the evidence to make it appear unreliable, or just have some fun with the gate guards. This area will provide an overview of all the topics we have discussed and possibly make sense of it all.

Only a few hackers ever work alone. These days, hacking is a business. Hacking organizations have offices; they have a management structure, and payroll systems. One could only wonder what health and retirement plans they offer employees. The organized hacking business has a fairly good communication system, partly thanks to encryption. You will also need a communication method that protects both yourself and the receiver from unwanted listeners. Whomever you will be working with, you will be introduced to methods for better protection. If your cellphone becomes a piece of evidence, this lesson will show you how to disable tracking mechanisms and SIM card intercept. We will discuss SIM card modifications and using the Advanced Encryption Standard (AES) to safely send and receive VOIP on a cellular line.

You will be introduced to the weapons used on the battlefield. Why show up for a gunfight with a knife? This section will cover the latest and greatest commercial and open source forensic software used. Along the way, we will touch on methods to bypass commercial firewalls, IDSs, behavior management tools, and other bumps in the road. You do not want to leave traces of your activities, or more importantly, show them how you bypassed their expensive equipment. It will be useful knowledge to know the weaknesses of forensic tools and ways to exploit those issues.

To conclude our lesson, we will walk you through the most effective steps you might need to infiltrate systems. Once inside, you will be guided through methods to enter systems undetected, conduct your mission, leave a backdoor, clean up the logs and activity trackers, and then exit without being noticed.

Feed Your Head: What Do You Need to Become a Digital Forensic Investigator?

Knowing how to find things is really the same thing as knowing how to hide them. If you're interested in being a forensic investigator, you'll need a good knowledge of general computer skills such as hardware, software, various operating systems, applications, and networks. You must be inquisitive and able to explore areas of a network or system that would make other folks queasy. Quick action and quick response must be balanced against patience in order to deal with the two aspects of digital forensics. They are:

Live Examination: this is where the digital evidence is still operational, has not been turned off, and the collection device is accessible for examination.

Post Mortem: the crime has already been committed. Evidence could be anywhere, so your job is that much harder since the bad guy could have used counter-forensic techniques to foil the investigation. Post mortem (Latin for "after death") usually means that the electronic device that could contain evidence has been turned off before you arrived.

Since you are a well trained examiner, you already know that you must follow a defined process to collect, analyze and protect the digital evidence.

Most investigators pursue professional certifications or training available from a variety of sources. While these may enhance expert witness credibility, this is not an absolute demand since there is no substitute for experience.

The Magically Disappearing Data Trick (Where and How to Hide Data)

Suppose for a minute that you just stumbled on (hacked into) a site with very special information. Let your imagination play with the idea of "special information." Whatever that information is, you happen to grab a copy of it. Nice job.

So, here you are with several megabytes of information on your computer. Where are you planning to store it all? Keeping it on your computer is not recommended. With your imagination already engaged, suppose there are eighty-five armed law enforcement agents heading towards your house. These agents have mean attack dogs, a helicopter with guns, and none of them has had their morning cup of coffee yet. Not even the dogs. You need to make that special information magically disappear, and quick.

First Things First – Large Data Sets

You can have all the (borrowed) data you want on your computer (not a smart move) as long as you use strong encryption so it isn't in plain text anymore. A better idea would be to put that incriminating information behind a secret revolving bookcase. You do have a secret revolving bookcase, don't you? Alright, we'll move that encrypted data somewhere else since you are the only person who doesn't have a secret revolving bookcase. The secret revolving bookcases are on sale, by the way. Buy two if you can.

An old trick to store incriminating data is to put it on someone's computer, presumably without their knowledge. Many other hackers use this same technique, since it allows them to place the burden of proof on the shoulders of law enforcement. It is difficult to find a person guilty of a computer crime if that person doesn't have any evidence that links them to the crime.

Let's get back to those cops, angry dogs and helicopters with guns heading your way. Before you found that one site with the special data, you may have located a few other servers that didn't interest you. For example, those three servers for "Diapers International" had low security, plenty of spare room, and small spurts of activity. (There's a joke in there somewhere, trust us).

Go back to "Diapers International" and take a peek at their server package. If anything smells suspicious, get out fast. Otherwise, look for a directory that is either used frequently or hardly used at all. Both types of directory activity have their advantages and disadvantages.

In an active directory, you can create multiple subdirectories and store your data without the transfer of data being noticed as much. The size of the data load should not set off any alarms because that main directory is in constant use. The bad news is that directory could be watched more closely than others due to its value to the organization. That active location is most likely being backed up on a regular basis. You don't want additional copies of your valuable data (evidence) floating out there.

Inactive or dead directories are popular spots to hide data. These locations may have served a purpose to the organization at some point.

This is where you will want to create a maze of subdirectories or set up a hidden directory. If you go with the maze, create a mental map of how you are going to navigate this maze to store your data. The idea is to build a pattern of subdirectories that you will store your encrypted data in. That pattern of storage needs to confuse anyone who locates your stash but you will know exactly what that pattern is. For example, if you build a directory under a few other directories, start branching off additional sublevels. For each sublevel or tree branch, those will split off into more sublevels or branches. Your storage pattern might be something as simple as, left sublevel, right sublevel, right, right, left.

Feed Your Head: Where Digital Forensics Investigators Start

If you are called into a computer crime scene as a digital forensic examiner, your first few steps will set the course on whether the evidence will be useful or will be worthless. Let's look at an example of two different situations where a digital crime was committed.

In the first example, you are brought in to recover evidence from a running computer with a connection to the organizations network. There is reasonable suspicion to believe this computer was used by a suspect to organize and commit a crime against a competitor. To collect evidence, you must not shut down that computer until you have all volatile and non volatile memory imaged. The suspects hard-drive needs to be imaged in a way that won't alter the contents of that drive. The tricky part is: what do you do about the network that the computer is connected to? There may be evidence on the network servers, but you can't just kick off all of the users to gather evidence. The answer is to perform a live analysis on each server and examine the images somewhere else.

This next example involves a computer that has already been powered down before you arrive. Who shut down that computer and why? If the suspect shut off the computer, when was it last used? Here is where your experience will be needed since the suspect may have used counter-forensic techniques.

Other types of devices such as video cameras, cell phones, and touch pads will require specialized tools and training if you expect to recover evidence. Your own curiosity and experience with digital devices will help your understanding of how data is stored on each machine.

You Can't Get There From Here

A simple question you might be asking yourself is "how do I keep my socks from smelling so bad?" Sorry, we can't help with that one, El Stinko, but, we can show you how to move large amounts of data from your computer to the "Diapers International" without being noticed. The Internet Control Message Protocol (ICMP) is long forgotten protocol that has magical covert powers if hacked a bit.

When you scan a port, you are really sending a TCP SYN request (layer 4) to see if that port responds. A proper ping uses ICMP, which doesn't use ports. Although ICMP rests on top of the Internet Protocol (IP), it is not a layer four protocol. This comes in very handy when we get into the firewall and network traffic logging.

Firewalls operate at several levels of the OSI model, restricting or allowing data flow based on the criteria that is given. The higher the stack layer, the deeper the firewall can inspect the contents of each packet request. At the lower layers, the firewall can still intercept and control data movement but it doesn't know as much about the data as it does at the higher layers. This is where ICMP packets become fun ways to deliver content.

The technique is known as "ICMP Tunneling." Before we can do much with this covert communication, we need some software tools.

Software Tools

- Wireshark - www.wireshark.org/

- Hping - http://www.hping.org/

- Kali Linux - http://www.kali.org/

ICMP packets have plenty of room after the header to store data (roughly 41k per packet). The idea here is to handcraft ICMP packets loaded with your data and send them through a covert ICMP tunnel to the location you want. You can generate ICMP packets using hping or nping (from the nmap people) and insert your payload at the same time. With these ping tools, you can customize the Ethernet header, the IP header and the payloads.

Digging the Tunnel

Why should you have to do all the hard work? Why not have the server on the other end do some of the work for you? You will need to set up an ICMP tunnel between your computer and the storage server, you know that much. Now it's time to think like a hacker.

Exercises

8.1 The first thing you need to do is figure out how this technique works. Here's where you explore the value of one of the most valuable resources for hackers on the Internet: Youtube. Given the pace of change on the Web, there may be a new video site of the day by the time you read this; but given the strength of certain search-based businesses, it's likely Youtube may still be your primary video resource.

To see a demonstration of how the ICMP tunnel works, check for videos online- there's more than enough!

8.2 There are two sides to a tunnel: the server side and the client side. You'll see that the creator of the video promises to release the source code, but never did on Youtube (despite visitor pleas).

Now you need to find the source code, which has indeed been posted to the Internet. Find the code. One further hint: notice the author's name.

8.3 You would need to get the server-side code onto your target, and run it, for this to work. How could you get that code onto a target?

Once both of these daemons are running host to host, the server will begin sniffing for ICMP packets. You will be sending commands through the tunnel to the server using ping and the server will respond in turn with ping packets. The server daemon will begin collecting your packets and placing the data where you have instructed. If the data flow is large, the server will establish additional multiple pings. The client side daemon will receive transmission updates through the same type of sniffer used on the server.

Passing the Buck

With portable drives having ever-higher capacity and smaller sizes, physically hiding large amounts of data is straightforward; put the media in a safe place away from your house and your computer. When those agents and mean dogs break down your front door, expect them to search every place imaginable; even your underwear drawer. Consider the fact that these people search houses every day for a living. They know all the hiding spots. Don't hand the media to a friend for safe keeping either, that's just not cool.

Before you even think about places to hide your treasure, encrypt the media, the data, or both first. Try TrueCrypt. (Oh, wait, you can't. Now that's a fascinating story you should look up what happened to Truecrypt!)

Place the media in a sealed plastic bag, something that is weatherproof. Use a straw to suck the air out of the bag to reduce moisture content as well as size. Don't dig a hole in the ground near your house to bury the media because fresh dirt will look suspicious to the dogs and the agents. Instead, look for hiding spots that are high off the ground. People rarely look up for some odd reason. Just make sure you can get to that spot when you need to. Expect any tape you plan on using to secure the bag to fail. Use twist ties, zip ties, twine, shoestring, or other objects that will ensure your bag doesn't come loose and fly away.

A favorite hiding spot is anything near a police station or in a police station. There are very few good hiding spots inside a station but plenty near the outside. Use your imagination but also think logically about placing, recovering, and leaving the area without drawing attention to yourself. Your activates may be better suited for daytime, since the dark tends to alarm people more. Planting a bag in broad daylight, usually later in the afternoon, wouldn't draw nearly as much attention as it would in the evening.

Working From Home

Many organizations offer free cloud storage with nothing more than a valid email account. Some places will give you 50 GB of free online storage. Google, Apple, Microsoft and many others provide various amounts of free storage. These cloud services, using a one-time email account, can be useful locations to store data. All you have to do is clear out your browser cache each time you visit and/or go incognito with Chrome so there are no traces of your visits on your computer. Some of these cloud services will allow you to synchronize your computer files with the online account. Disable this function and remove all entries that point to the accounts. It is easier and safer to view your data through a web browser instead of using the cloud's interface.

Next Things Next – Small Bits of Bytes

If you have small amounts of data, like passwords, private keys, or a secret recipe for soup, you can slip that data into places that will not be noticed. Don't go so far as trying to hide data in your DNA, we've already tried that and it gave us the lousy sense of humor you are reading. Plus, we twitch a lot. There are better ways.

Malware creators have long known that there is storage space on Windows systems in the Master Boot Record (MBR). It's not much space but enough to hide a private key or a DLL. Your lunch bag will not fit in the MBR, so don't try it, we already did.

Swamped by Swaps

Swap files are places on a media drive that is temporary RAM. The swap file space allows the computer to run faster even if it runs out of RAM to execute programs. UNIX and Linux set aside a permanent block of media for swap storage. Even if the computer is turned off, this hard drive swap file space can still contain data from previous events.

Windows swap files (**page files**) can get quite large and hold pieces of recent files. This could be even more dangerous if you were connected to a windows based server. Windows servers store a significant amount of user data that can be handy to the forensic examiner. Take a look at "temp" directories for the swap files.

Give 'em Some Slack

Files are stored in **clusters**. Depending on the operating system, the clusters can vary in size. If you created a file on your computer, that file might only need 50% of the cluster's space. This leaves a cluster with open space left. This open space within a cluster is called **file slack** or just **slack** for short. If you delete a file that was in that partial cluster space, that space is still available even if the file was deleted.

The 50% cluster space that was previously occupied with a file, will keep that data intact. These data remnants remain in the cluster until it is filled with other data. Windows automatically creates slack space as soon as any file is created, viewed, modified, or saved.

File Makeovers

Some of the best places to hide data is to hide it in plain sight. File modification is just a fancy way of changing the name of a file, altering the extension of files, or changing the file attributes. By now, you should already know how to change the name of a file. You made a file "Evil Plans" earlier, now let's get creative. Would you put all of your passwords in a file and name that file "Passwords?" No, of course not. Nor should you put all of your work in files that can be easily identified.

When looking to modified files, look at file extensions. File compression is an easy way to cover tracks and save space, however, those files will be the first one the agents will be checking. So, you will need to alter the file extension. This can be accomplished by editing the last three characters of the file name.

Changing a .doc file to a .gif is as simple as changing an .odt file to a .avi. Creating the altered files can become tricky and time consuming. Look at file sizes, created dates, and modified dates to give you ideas of how to customize each file. An .odt file should not be a gigabyte in size, as well as an .avi file should not be a few kilobytes either. An .avi file should be several gigabytes in size.

Look at the file dates too. The files that were created or accessed within a week of the criminal event and after the event should ring a bell in your head. Alter those dates to any day at least a year before your hack. If you really want to have some fun, change the dates to impossible dates, such as 30 February or 21 March 2112. Don't forget Pi Day, using that date and time will really show who knows their math and who doesn't.

Exercises

8.4 The date is 21 December 2012. During a forensic examination you locate several files. Along with files you can see the size of the file and the file type. Digging deeper, you also notice the date those files were created and the last time each file was opened or modified. Look at each of the following files and see if any file looks suspicious.

Name of file	Type of file	Size of file	File creation date	Last time file was accessed or modified
Passwords.exe	Executable	13KB	May 2008	12/19/12
Fall 2012 vacation.jpg	Picture	12948KB	June 2009	12/19/12
Planstokillwife.doc	Word document	2KB	December 2012	12/20/12
Love songs.mp3	Music file	7985340KB	Unknown	Unknown

Which of these files look suspicious?

Which files would you analyze first?

Are any of these files fakes?

Why did you chose your response for each file?

There will be many times in your life were you may think using a hammer will help solve computer hardware issues. A well-known tool store once sold a tool set called the "Ultimate Tool Kit," inside of which was a box of ten different types of hammers. In the field of forensics, hammers will not help you solve any cases. Using a hammer may create other challenges, possibly making you a suspect.

Feed Your Head: What Kind of Electronic Evidence Do Investigators Collect?

The key to analyzing storage media is this: when a file is deleted, it doesn't really go away. It's still there, on the storage media; just the file system entry for that file has been deleted. The data is still on drive. With a data recovery program, you can read the unallocated space or the slack space to see what data was deleted! Malicious software writers often hide their software in the slack space of files. Criminals often assume that, because they deleted all their "criminal" files, there is no evidence remaining. Many of those naive criminals are now in prison.

When we're doing a **digital forensic investigation**, we have to know where to look, how to protect it, what's important, and what it means to the crime. These are some common places to look for electronic evidence:

From Devices

- Office desktop computers/workstations

- Network servers

- Home computers/personal USB drives/cdroms/dvds/portable media devices

- Laptops, netbooks

- PDAs, tablets, audio players

- Cell phones/smart phones/portable hot spots

- Fax machines, photocopiers

Your Printer Will Give You Up

Fax machines and photocopiers have memory inside these devices. A fax machine will usually have RAM while a photocopier will have both RAM and a fairly large hard drive. Both of these machines record the time and date of events and much more data. The copiers hard drive keeps a digital copy of every document that passed through it. These days the photocopier can scan, fax, print, and connect to a network for easier access. All of this data is stored on the internal hard drive.

From Backups

- System-wide backups (monthly/weekly/incremental)

- Disaster recovery backups (stored off site)

- Personal or "ad hoc" backups (look for CDs/DVDs, USB drives and other portable media)

- Cloud storage accounts

Digital Evidence

Digital evidence is defined as any information of value in a court of law that is either stored or transmitted in a digital form. It is information gathered from digital storage media, network information, or duplicate copies of data found during forensic investigations. Digital evidence includes files such as:

- Graphic files

- Audio and video recording files

- Internet browser histories

- Server/system event, security, and audit logs

- Word processing and spreadsheet files

- Email

- Registries

- Cellphone system data

- Firewall, router, and IDS log files

The data and devices you find as evidence will also be the same data that can be manipulated to hide information from you. Roll your sleeves up because we'll be getting into data concealment and counter-forensic techniques soon.

Finally, digital evidence must have certain characteristics to be used in court. Those characteristics are:

Admissible: evidence must be related to the fact being proven.

Authentic: evidence must be real and related to the incident in a proper way.

Complete: evidence must prove the entirety of the activity.

Reliable: evidence must have proven authenticity and veracity (truthfulness).

Believable: evidence must be clear and understandable by the judges in court.

> **Know the Law First**
>
> There are legal requirements that must be met before any evidence collection can begin. Please consult with your organization's legal department, or catch up on your country's latest legal standards.

The Disappearing Data Magic Trick (Making Data Irrecoverable)

Behind these two doors we have option 1, which is digital sanitation and option 2, physical destruction of media. Each option has merit, but it will be up to you as to which method you want to use. The folks here at Hacker Highschool love the sound of an electric drill boring holes into old hard drives. If you put that sound to music, you would have an outstanding remix. However, if you can't bear to see or hear holes plunged violently into hardware, we have media sanitation to remove, unwanted data. A kinder, gentler way of blasting the heck out of unwanted data bits.

After you have been using a hard drive or any other type of digital storage device, you will probably get to the point where it doesn't serve a useful purpose. It is a really awful idea to throw that media in the trash or give it to someone who might use it again unless your data is removed first. Do you really want someone finding that jpeg of you in your Batman costume last year? What about those old receipts from your last part-time job? Would you want those homemade videos of you dancing in your underwear to end up on that video site? Well, let's get rid of those worrisome digital memories on that old media before you pass it along to someone else.

Wash, Rinse, Repeat

Sanitizing media is inexpensive (not very much fun) and provides secure destruction of sensitive data. You can eradicate data, wiping those digits off the face of the earth using open source software. One of the simplest methods is to encrypt your media using True Crypt. Once the entire physical chunk of storage is encrypted, it is now somewhat safe to toss that hardware away. The logic is that the entire data image cannot be decrypted unless you provide the passphrase. Pretty simple, right? If those eighty-five agents get their hands on your old media, it is useless to them since you are the only person who can unlock the data. If another person obtains your old media, they will have to reformat and repartition it before it can be used.

There are roughly two standards for proper media destruction. The first one is US DOD 5220.22-M and the other is the Gutmann algorithm. DOD 5220.22 is a US National Industrial Security Program Operating Manual that provides instruction on destruction of data. The U.S. Department of Defense like to destroy things too, so they only authorize complete destruction as a means to remove data.

The Gutmann algorithm, named after Dr. Peter Gutmann and Colin Plumb, gives a little more latitude on physical annihilation of hardware. The algorithm requires the media to be overwritten thirty-five times in a manufacture specific pattern. Different drives require different overwrite patterns. Although this method is an outstanding researched backed technique, it has been outdated due to the size of newer drives and built-in controller settings.

More Software Tools

Within the open source community, there are some great software tools will make your data impossible to recover. The software will not damage your media but will make the data on it unrepairable. When running the software you press the "start" button, don't expect to ever see that data again. Not even in the afterlife.

Boot and Nuke

http://www.Dban.org

Boot and Nuke comes as an ISO image that you burn to a CD and boot your system off of it. Once the software is up and running, you just select which drive you want sanitized (Nuked). Dban is an industry standard for bulk data destruction and emergency uses. Once Dban has been used on a drive, there is no forensic recovery possible. That data is gone, bye-bye.

Eraser

http://sourceforge.net/projects/eraser/files/latest/download

This program is strictly made for Windows. Even though Window Vista on up has ability to format and write ones over the media, Eraser formats the drive and writes random data over the drive many times. The program does this function several times, format, write, format write and so on until a pattern is completed.

Sderase

http://sourceforge.net/projects/sderase/?source=directory

SD is a newcomer to disk wiping, just released August 28th 2012. The programs creator made an interesting comment on the web site. SDerase proclaims that it meets US DOD 5220.22-M data sanitation requirements. US DOD 5220.22-M mandates that the only acceptable method for media and data removal is physical destruction of the media. We have yet to see any software that can perform physical damage.

Hammer, Drill, Bigger Hammer

The one method that has stood the test of time for media eradication; the one method that all experts agree on its success, is physical destruction. Smash it, pound it, pulverize it, or tear it apart. Use your imagination to find ways of ruining media. A magnet will only work on magnetic material, so flash drives will just laugh at you if you put a speaker magnet next to it. The laughing media will certainly pause to reflect its pending doom when you show up with a hammer, though.

A typical carpenter's hammer will apply approximately a lot of damage to any solid object it impacts. Larger hammers apply larger amounts of damage (and fun). Keep your thumbs clear. A rock can perform the same function as a hammer, on your thumb and on the media you want to destroy. From a Return on Investment (ROI) perspective, a rock is more economical but can require continuous replacement with long-term use.

Likewise, an electric drill using a large bit can produce excellent demolition results. The best method for drilling destruction is to drill several holes in various places on the media. There are additional hazards involved with using a drill that must be considered:

- Wear safety glasses or similar eye protection

- Do not try and hold the media in your lap while you drill

- Do not try and hold the media in your hand while you drill

- Do not ask a friend or family member to hold the media in their lap or hands while you drill

- To reduce damage to your drill and drill bit, place cardboard or wood under the media before drilling

Once you are done turning your old media into tiny pieces, your next step will be to spread the parts over several garbage cans. Grab a slingshot and practice hitting cans with the remaining parts. Make an art project out of the ruins. There are all sorts of ways to separate the small parts over a large area. You might as well have fun scattering them.

Planting a Garden

To survive in this line of work, you need to be a bit paranoid. Okay, a lot paranoid. Being alert and planning ahead is a good idea and not something to be taken lightly (this same advice can be applied towards early retirement planning). In the physical world, we leave hair strands, fibers from our clothes, fingerprints, shoe prints, and other evidence of our presence. Unlike the physical world, it is possible to enter a digital area, spend some time playing around, and exit that area without leaving a single piece of evidence that you were ever there. Consider how this can work for better and for worse – and exactly how bad it could be, to be on the wrong side of this process.

We will cover the whole process later on, but here we are going to focus on hiding your tracks. In networking there are two types of devices. The first device is basically a "dumb" device, which means that the device doesn't keep a log of activities. These devices are common switches, hubs, bridges, and so forth. They just do whatever it is they were designed to do.

On the other side, we have "intelligent" devices that do keep logs of certain activities and can invoke decisions based on the filters and configurations that are installed. These devices fall into the category of firewalls, routers, range extenders, servers, and other network hardware that keeps track of data flow. These are the devices that you will need to pay attention to because they are the ones that will monitor, record, and possibly disrupt your hack. These network roadblocks are covered in depth at other HHS lessons.

You need to know how to deal with these devices to cover your tracks and if needed, lead those eight-five agents somewhere else. In your planning, it might help to work backwards on a timeline. This allows you to set the amount of time you will be in that network and minimize the chances of you being caught by controlling your exposure time.

Seeding the Garden

You will need to consider multiple ways to properly cover your tracks, before you exit the target network. If you just depend on a single method, such as erasing all log files, you are leaving yourself open to other tracking methods. Erasing log files may sound like a super idea but what happens if there are hidden redundant logs? Oops. We need to choose several courses of action that complement each other but do not interfere with your overall plans. Consider these points from the perspective of the investigator – and that of the perpetrator.

Planting logic bombs have been used in the past by outsourced vendors who haven't been paid, angry admins, and ransom-minded folks. Each of those examples place logic bombs where maximum damage to data will occur. Complete network data destruction is not a great idea if you want to keep a low profile after a network breech. A logic bomb that will simply delete or corrupt log files if triggered by an audit within so many days (five) or hours after your exit, would work well to cover your tracks and not alarm too many people.

CCleaner (http://www.ccleaner.com/)is a free Windows-based program that has consistently performed well for home and commercial users. (It was originally called Crap Cleaner but when they suddenly went big time they realized they'd have to have a more respectable name.) With this 332 KB utility, you can select which log files you want to delete or edit on any machine you have admin access to. You can even clear your browser history, erasing you own tracks once your job is complete. CCleaner will try to make a system restore point before it alters anything. Your two choices are to not allow a restore point or look for a file in the root directory labeled "cc_20110928_203957" or something like that. Remove and delete that file before leaving, even if that file is on your own drive.

Root kits hide activity and is valuable for Linux-based servers that do not have many security holes to use.

Feed Your Head: Digital Forensics Principles

Like any science, digital forensics relies on well-defined methods, which are basically concerned with keeping evidence intact. Consider this logic: if you've lost control of your evidence, even for a minute, it's not evidence any more – it may have been altered.

Data files can be altered without seeming so. It is easy to change the date, check sum, and last access dates after someone has edited a file or a log. One of the forensic investigator's duties is to prove that the evidence collected has not been altered in any way. Basically, you will need to prove that nothing has happened to that data while it was collected, analyzed, in custody and at all times.

This is why it is important to use proven procedures to collect, inspect, and handle all data. One simple mistake could render all your hard work worthless. This is where a good technique comes into play. By conducting each investigation in the same manner and using the same process to document your actions, you can prove that nothing has tampered with your evidence.

Digital Forensic Methodology

Digital forensics is a branch of criminology, so it's all about a procedural collection of legally useful evidence. This means that you are only looking for evidence that matches the crime, not poking around just because you can. The following figure shows the steps you'd take in helping a criminal investigation.

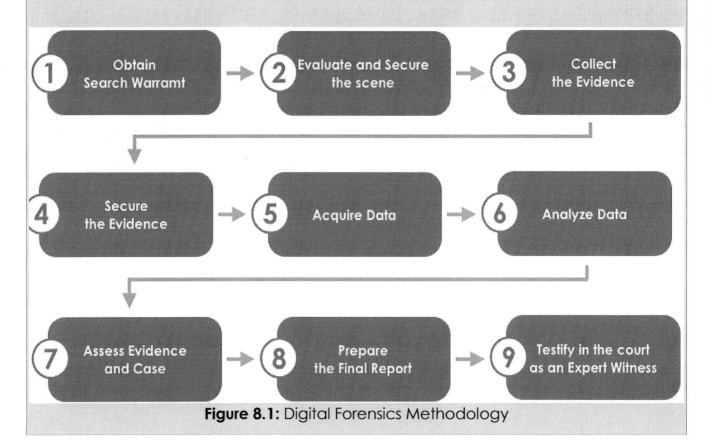

Figure 8.1: Digital Forensics Methodology

Digital Forensics Process

When you're investigating a computer crime, you need to base your work on a process, such as a policy, procedures, and checklists. Your forensic process must be repeatable and hold up to scrutiny by other forensic experts. You should develop an investigative process that requires constant documentation of everything action that evidence goes through. If it isn't documented, it didn't happen.

An example of this process is:

1. Identification of evidence (must be documented)

2. Collection of evidence (must be documented in Chain of Custody)

3. Preservation of evidence (must be documented in Chain of Custody)

4. Analysis or interpretation (of course, must be documented)

5. Communication of your findings and documentation

Probably the most critical single document will be the **Chain of Custody** documents, which should state exactly what has been taken as evidence, by whom, and who has subsequent custody. Lose custody of your evidence, even for a few minutes, and it's probably worthless now.

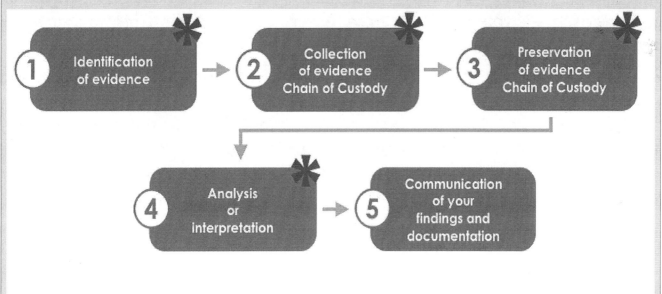

* **must be documented**

Figure 8.2: *Digital Forensic Process*

> **Evidence gets lost all the time!**
>
> Don't let all your hard work become wasted because a piece of vital information wasn't labeled or never made it through your Chain of Custody procedures. Unlike your teachers, a judge will not accept "my dog ate my forensic evidence" as an excuse for something missing.
>
> On the other hand, lost evidence may be a wonderful thing, depending on your perspective.

This is an Exercise for Anyone Interested in Criminal Justice

Police criminal records are stored on local servers, usually housed in the main headquarters with a backup file system stored at a satellite police station. Within the primary criminal records database, there are several subsets of information. These subsets are where daily investigative data is kept, individual background history (arrest warrants, recent prior offenses), results of forensic test requests,

As with the FBI's criminal mainframe, there isn't any public accessible link via the Internet. These workstations can access the Internet themselves though. Communication links are available through workstations in the police buildings, with privileges granted based on job function. Along with the workstations, police vehicles are equipped with remote communication encrypted laptops. These vehicle computers are highly capable with access to most of the typical police databases and the Internet.

Currently, these portable computers remain on even when the vehicle is turned off for short amounts of time. Communications are handled through wireless data networking operating on the "Part 90 private and public Land Mobile Radio (LMR) two-way radio system licensees operating legacy wideband (25 kHz) voice dispatch or data/supervisory control and data acquisition radio systems in the 150-174 MHz (VHF) and 421-512 MHz (UHF). The FCC has mandated these frequency bands must make the transition to the narrowband technology (12.5 kHz or less) by January 2013.

Exercise

8.5 This narrowbanding is causing a major cost crunch for many law enforcement agencies since a great majority of them invested in frequency hopping radios. Frequency hopping allows a radio to "hop" across a spectrum of radio frequencies, making it difficult to jam or intercept. Each radio is set to "hop" based on a master radio and the time, plus or minus 3 seconds. Once the slave radio if synchronized to the master radio, all transmissions will sound perfectly normal, even as the radios bounce through 70 frequencies a minute. Narrowbanding shuts down this hopping capability, since the radios are restricted to only a few channels. Can you find out what frequencies are used in your area?

Local law enforcement agencies have established Public Utility Contracts (PUCs) with major wireless carriers to provide data usually through the entire range of their jurisdiction. The wireless frequencies are the same as your typical data cellular device, EDGE, 2G, 3G, and 4G LTE. The only difference in data transmission is the SSL encryption used between the servers and the mobile computers. Programs like Snort and Wireshark work well to intercept data packets, however, the computer needs to be stationary or the police have to be chasing after you.

Earlier we talked about hiding things near police stations. There is another reason to hang around a police station, especially the motor pool where the cruisers are parked. This is perfect location for packet capturing of login and password credentials. When the police vehicle is first unlocked and prepared for the next patrol shift, the onboard computer must be authenticated and synchronized to the data servers. This is performed at the beginning of every shift change, since one police officer is replacing another police officer.

Another recent implementation to the mobile computers, VOIP has been added. The primary purpose of this addition was to stop interception of police radio transmissions by bad guys and nosy reporters. VOIP is whole other system wrought with vulnerabilities.

Home Away from Home, or When Business Gets Too Personal

One major flaw in the law enforcement community is their use of email, both on and off duty. The use of cell phones for personal calls, emails forwarded to home accounts, Facebook and other communications has blurred the lines of "official business." FBI agents take work home with them all the time, just as police officers do. Getting that work data in and out of the office is as simple as a mouse click, for anyone.

Consider this, most email user names start with some combination of first name, last name, separated by a dot and followed by the agencies address. This would look like First.Last@police.state. Gov. Let's say the email address you want is for police officer Dean Martin with the New York State police department. That email address would be D.martin@troopers.ny.gov. Each police department publicly displays their URL on their web site, usually under "Contact Us" or "Complaints."

In many cases, the first portion of their email address will be the officer's user name. Where this comes in handy is the open sharing of information between other law enforcement agencies. Once you have gained access to one email account, it is easier to intercept those communications and move towards the active investigation database.

One problem will be with accessing the databases. This access is controlled by a need to know and access is only granted to those areas the officer is working on. If you log in as one agent and attempt to access a part of a database that agent should not have access to, red flags will go off. This all goes back to the reconnaissance portion of your hack. Know as much as you can about who is doing what with your case.

There several flavors of security/forensics distributions of Linux on the Internet. Consider going to **www.securitydistro.com** and trying several. Before you go trying some of these software kits on your parents computer, read the documentation. Each software package contains powerful elements that can easily ruin your day if not properly executed. Granted, the whole idea behind hacking is to learn by trying. Just be careful, be educated and never forget that your actions have effects on others. Someday YOU will be the "other."

Software Tools and Collections

The most common digital forensics/security testing open source or free software is in collections of tools such as:

- **Kali Linux** (www.kali.org/)

- **Sleuthkit** (www.sleuthkit.org)

- **Katana** (sourceforge.net/projects/katana-usb/)

- **CAINE** (www.caine-live.net/)

- **Wireshark** (www.wireshark.org/)

- **DEFT** (www.deftlinux.net/)

- **HELIX** (https://www.e-fense.com/store/index.php?_a=viewProd&productId=11)

- **UNetBootin** (http://unetbootin.sourceforge.net/)

Exercises

8.6 Head over to any one of the forensic software providers listed above. Follow the directions to create your own live CD. The word "live" means that the media can boot up your computer and load its own operating system without needing to use the one already installed on that machine.

8.7 Now use UnetBootin to make a bootable USB drive loaded with the same forensic tools. Remember that these tools are running on Linux (various flavors) so don't worry about compatibility with the operating system you are already using.

8.8 Play around with the software tools and read the documentation. While you are at it, mount your own hard drive and attempt to recover any files that you might have deleted recently. Once you recover a deleted file, rename that file to "Evil Plans" using the same file extension it already had. You'll be using that "Evil Plans" file later on.

8.9 Many of the software packages have graphical user interfaces (GUIs) and some run using the command line. Take a close look at those programs that run from the command line. Notice how the switches (/s) at the end of each command can create powerful tools within themselves.

Data Media Analysis

Computer forensics investigators use various software tools for analyzing and recovering data on various forms of media. There are two basic reasons to conduct a forensic analysis: to reconstruct an attack after it occurred, and to examine a device that may have been used to carry out a crime.

The first step before proceeding with any type of data analyze is to make an exact image of the evidence and to only work with that image. The software tools mentioned earlier allow investigators to perform the following tasks and more:

- Search for text on media devices in file space, slack space, and unallocated space
- Find and recover data from files that have been deleted or hidden
- Find data in encrypted files
- Repair FAT (FAT16, FAT32, eFAT) partition tables and boot records
- Recover data from damaged NTFS partitions (often Linux can do this when Windows can't)
- Joined and split files
- Analyze and compare files
- Clone devices that hold data
- Make data images and backups
- Erase confidential file securely
- Edit files using a hex editor
- Crack certain encrypted folders and files
- Alter file attributes or remove restrictive permissions (read or write only)

Time for a Date

Getting in Time With Offset

Event time is usually crucial, so the **offset** between the time of the system from which evidence has been taken and atomic time should be recorded (don't forget the timezone!). Typically, this is done AFTER evidence has been secured since it involves starting the system.

Knowing when an event happened or didn't happen is a crucial fact that must be established for each piece of evidence. If a suspect admits that they "never sent a threatening email" to the victim, your job will be to locate that email and confirm when it was sent and by whom. Throughout this lesson we will convey this same message until we think you've had enough. Then, we will bring it up one more time, just to be sure you are sick of hearing it.

EXIF Data

Digital photos are encoded with **metadata** known as EXIF or Exchangeable File Image File Format. The original idea of using EXIF was to offer photographers precise data on each photo, such as shutter speed, color balance, and time and date of the photo. The amazing array of information includes even more additional data if the camera has a GPS activated, including location services.

Most of the cameras that input this tracking data are cell phones. Cell phone cameras include in the EXIF personal data about the users name and if the phones GPS is operating, the EXIF will provide the location where the photo was taken.

Granted, all this information can be spoofed however, few people know about this metadata in the first place. One picture posted in a social media sight can be enough to locate your suspect.

Imaging Tools

Just as with hard disks, any data storage media that could be evidence should be imaged and then stored, so your analysis work is only done on the image. You never want to work directly with the original evidence because doing so could alter the information on that media. Each of the forensic software collections mentioned above can create an exact image of most forms of media. If your forensic lab computer can read the media, those software tools can image it.

> Use hashing techniques to ensure that the binary image is an exact bit-for-bit copy of the original. Take a hash of the original. Create the image, and then take a hash of the image. If the two hashes are the same, you have an identical copy. This should be performed by the same software we discussed earlier. It's no use to work on an image that isn't the exact same as the original evidence.

Give Them the Boot(ing)

Booting is the process by which a small program actually initializes the operating system installed on a computer or on the booting device. Part of this process involves looking into the boot sector to find out where the operating system is. USB drives can become a boot device as can a CD/DVD, ZIP drives, flash media cards, and network interface card (using PXE).

A "live" CD/DVD/USB or other media means the device can boot up the computer. As long as the computer BIOS allows for booting from other media, this bootable media can load all sorts of operating systems including virtual machines and dual booting.

The ability to boot from several types of media can allow a suspect to boot a computer with their own operating system and store all their evidence on that same device. This form of boot-up would not leave any trace of activity on the suspect's computer and would make your job all that much more difficult.

Deleted Data

A killer usually wants to get rid of the dead body and the weapon they used as quickly as possible after the crime. The killer wants to destroy any evidence that would link them to the murder. A computer crime suspect will want to do the exact same thing. Digital evidence can be removed easier and quicker if the suspect knows what they are doing. (Don't take this as an invitation to commit "the perfect crime." We guarantee there is no such thing. Honest. We would know.)

To delete traces of old files, Linux uses the command **dd**

```
dd if=/dev/zero of=/home/filename
sync
rm /home/filename
sync
```

But dd if=/dev/zero of=/home/filename runs forever! Or until you terminate it. Try this instead:

```
cat /dev/zero | head -c $((1024*1024)) > /home/filename
```

This creates a file of exactly 1 MB (1024 times 1024 bytes)

To delete files and remove traces of those files in Windows:

1. Using Explorer, select the files or folders and hit the "delete" key.

2. Clear all files in Temp directory or use software like CCleaner.

3. Once the files are deleted, select the Recycle Bin.

4. Right click on the Recycle Bin and select "Empty Recycle Bin."

5. Create a new Restore Point under "Systems" and delete the older Restore Points.

6. Reboot.

CCleaner lets you select which log files you want to delete or edit on any machine you have admin access to. A suspect can even clear their browser history, erasing their own tracks once their job is complete. CCleaner will try to make a system restore point before it alters anything. Your two choices are to not allow a restore point or look for a file in the root directory labeled "cc_20110928_203957" or something like that. A suspect will remove and delete that file before leaving, even if that file is on a portable drive.

Feed Your Head: Video May Save You – or Convict You

Could a digital video camera solve one crime and yet be part of another crime? Yes. On 5 August 2012, two jet skiing tourists collided in Waikiki, Hawaii. The accident killed a 16-year-old California girl. Honolulu Police had a difficult time collecting evidence since there were only a few eyewitnesses. The other jet ski rider claimed he was sitting on his jet ski and didn't see the victim until the mishap.

One eyewitness mentioned to the police that someone had a video camera and was filming the scene when it happened. The video camera was actually being used by the perpetrator's girlfriend, who was filming the jet skiing boyfriend.

When the Honolulu Police asked for the video camera, that mishap segment was missing. Forensic examination revealed the deleted data, showing the boyfriend riding in a dangerous and reckless manner by standing up and speeding when he struck the deceased girl from behind.

The girlfriend later admitted to deleting the video data to keep her friend out of trouble. The suspect pleaded "No contest" to the charges, while his girlfriend is awaiting possible criminal charges for "tampering with evidence" and "impeding a criminal investigation."

Formatting Media

Most media needs to be formatted before it can be used for a particular operating system. As a rule of thumb, formatting destroys all data that was previously on that media. If you come across a hard drive or other media that was recently formatted. It may contain evidence that the suspect wants to remove. With the software tools listed earlier, you have the capabilities to recover files and folder from that media.

There are programs out there that will format the media, write random information on the new formatted drive, reformat and continue this process as many times as you wish. Under these extreme conditions, recovering the original files and folders will be quite difficult. The key to recovering anything is to identify this event and media as quickly as possible.

Precautions While Collecting Evidence from a Data Storage Device

These are the rules for when you're on the opposite side: when it comes to collecting media for forensic examination. You will not need a hammer or a drill. In this situation, you will need to be careful and non-destructive.

- Hold the media only by outer edges and avoid scratches or dropping it.
- Use water-based markers for writing on evidence.
- Place digital evidence devices in a waterproof and labeled bag.
- Take special precautions with storage media that are cracked or damaged.
- Do not rinse media with water to remove surface dirt, possible drug contamination, grease, an/or oils.
- Do not use any type of cleaner based on organic or petroleum solvents near the evidence.
- Create an image of the data on the media and work with the image to prevent damage to the original data.

Exercise

8.10   While analyzing a suspect's 4 gig xd card you notice that the partition shows a 2.5 gig logical partition and nothing else. On the xd card you locate family pictures, routine documents and other mundane data. You do notice one encrypted file that is using 192 bit AES block cipher inside a folder named "kids pix."

Why is the xd card only 2.5 gigs when it should be 4 gigs?

Does it concern you that there is an encrypted file located in a strange folder?

What do you know about AES and what does a 192 bit block cipher mean to you during your forensic investigation?

Can you crack this file?

Steganography: A look at security controversy

The topic of steganography gives you a chance to look at how differently security experts can think. It is a totally workable means to secretly transfer data; it's just never been found in the wild. Is anybody using this stuff?

Steganography: It's Real, It's Easy and It Works

When you're performing digital forensic investigations, it is not enough to simply recover photos, documents, videos, audio and VoIP packet data contained on the suspect media without also testing that evidence for potential hidden evidence such as steganography. While it may appear to be a benign picture, that picture may contain a plethora of hidden information.

Steganography, often referred to as **stego**, is the ability to hide information within transmissions without anyone being able to notice any change or modification to the original host without the use of special software tools. For example, a picture containing a hidden stego message looks identical to the casual viewer and gives no obvious indications that any modifications have been made to the original. While similar to encryption in that stego is used to hide objects and data, making it unnoticeable and unreadable, stego but should not be confused with cryptography. Steganography embeds the information in such things as documents or images while cryptography encrypts the information using a cypher or encryption key that is used to scramble and later unscramble the message.

In a recent case, stego was used, and detected by the FBI. Ten stego criminals were then released to Russia as part of a modern day spy swap. You can read more about that online.

Steganography uses many different techniques from data insertion to algorithmic but to make the concept easier to understand let's just say that steganography inserts data into a host file in a manner that does not readily change the host file that can then be distributed to other persons who can then reconstruct the hidden message(s) contained in that host file. While graphics, bitmap images in particular are the most commonly used steganography hosts, the host can be audio files, videos, or documents as well.

There are more than 600 known stego creation and detection tools available on the Internet. But even with all the tools, a person who is trained to use a hex editor can readily detect steganography "infected" hosts if they have access to a library of clean original images, documents, videos and audio files with which to compare the suspect hosts against. Steganography detection is also aided with the usage of Steganography signature libraries similar to anti-virus definition detection as well as the comparison of steganography based hash values. Steganography hash values are available at sites such as http://www.hashkeeper.org or http://www.stegoarchive.com

A few examples of common steganography creation tools include **S-Toolsv4, JP Hide-and-Seek, JStegShell, ImageHide, ES Stego** and **Dounds Stegonagraphy**. Whereas **StegDetect** and **Stegbreak** are tools used to help detect steganography infected hosts. For more information about Steganography you can visit http:// Stegano.net

Exercises

Steganography Retrieval Techniques

8.11　　　Obtain a copy of Dound's Steganography.

8.12　　　Create and encode a message.

1. Locate a .bmp image, and save the image to the desktop.

2. Launch Dound's Steganography. To have 32-bit color settings, refer to the "how to use" file that comes with the program. The settings must be in place for the program to work properly.

3. Click the File tab, select Open, navigate to the saved .bmp image, and click Open. The image appears in the image field below the Message field.

4. Type the text message of your choice to be hidden in the Message field.

5. Click the Function tab, and select Encode Message, which will encode—hide—the data behind the photo. After the encoding is complete, the message Encoding Complete appears. Click Ok.

6. Click the File tab, and select Save As. Give the file a unique name, and select the location to save the file.

7. Close the program and then reopen it.

8. Click the File tab, and select Open. Navigate to the file with the hidden data, and select Open. The .bmp image will appear in the image field.

9. Click the Function tab, and select Decode Message. The hidden text will be decoded and displayed in the Message field.

8.13   Demonstrate how to hide data behind an image file.

1. Locate a .bmp image.

2. Use Dound's Steganography to open the image.

3. Enter data in the Dound's Steganography message box.

4. Encode the .bmp image you located in Step 1 with hidden data.

5. Save the file.

6. Email the file to another student.

8.14   Open image Emailed to you from other student(s), and decode their hidden text.

1. Were you able to hide your text message using Dound's Steganography and encode the image?

2. Was the other student able to open, decode, and view your hidden text?

3. Were you able to discover or decode their text message?

Or, for a completely alternate point of view, read on.

Steganography Is a Scam

A reviewer who is now paying us not to reveal his name had this to say (this is why we keep reminding you to think twice about what you post/email/text):

> I want to state my protest of having Steganography as a portion of Counter Forensics. After reading countless papers, articles and crap on the subject, I think there are so many easier ways to hide data. In 2009, the U.S. Department of Justice funded an eight month investigation into locating terrorist messages in pornography. The investigation was funded to the University of Texas. At the end of eight months, it was reported with great satisfaction that over 130,000 pornographic images were analyzed for terrorist messages but none actually had any hidden text. The entire investigation relied on 18 postgraduate students to pore over every Internet porn site they could locate. The investigators were all male.
>
> What I understood from all this money was that we ended up with a bunch of horny college students and no useful data. In case you were wondering, the Department of Homeland Security and the U.S. Air Force replicated the same type of study (independent of each other and totally unaware that the same study had already been performed) looking for hidden messages in dirty pictures. Each study found nothing except one message was found in a small batch. Those pictures were deemed to be a hoax by someone trying to see if hiding messages in dirty picture was a worthy prospect. I swear!
>
> Steganography is a bunch of horse pucky unless you guys know something that I don't. The topic is used to fill up spaces in otherwise empty security books. I don't want to fall prey to the same stupid material. I've even interviewed one of the world's leading scientists on the topic and he didn't convince me.

Personally we are delighted with this kind of controversy. First, of course, it simply gets people thinking. And then come the questions: Were these all-male testing crews just capitalizing on the opportunity to look at porn all day? For pay? The fact that three different organizations did these "studies" sounds like it might support this notion. But even further, was porn even the right kind of pictures to test?

Exercise

8.15   What would be a better type of picture or media for sending stego messages? Where would be the ideal place to share it? Make it so.

Windows Forensics

Windows can be its own worst enemy when it comes to maintaining data. The operating system is a resource hog, fills up a hard drive, and never seems to sit idle. How are you expected to examine an engine spark-plug in a car moving at a high rate of speed with no chance of the car slowing down? Oh, and Windows is constantly moving files around and modifying them, even the ones you are looking for.

We'll start this messy affair by covering the different types of volatile and non volatile information an investigator can collect from a Windows system. This section goes into more details about grabbing and analyzing data in memory, the registry, events, and files.

Laptops Are Treasure Troves

Some forensic cases will involve a data breach. The latest historical data shows that laptop incidents caused the highest loss of corporate data than any other form. Hacking was far behind laptop theft with hacking breeches only accounting for 16% of all reported breeches. What does this mean to you?

Laptops are often issued to employees without much accountability or restrictions. This would be like handing out the keys to company cars and not caring who drove which car where. The results of such negligence is a whole bunch of company laptops being misplaced, forgotten, or taken without any oversight. Those same laptops are usually set up for remote access into the enterprise server. It could be your job to determine how a bad guy was able to access the organizations network. Missing laptops might be your answer.

Keep this in mind as well, when you lose YOUR laptop. What could people find out from your laptop? How happy would you be about it?

Volatile Information

Volatile information is information that is lost when a system is powered down or otherwise loses power. Volatile information exists in physical memory or RAM, and consists of information about processes, network connections, open files, clipboard contents etc. This information describes the state of the system at a particular point in time.

When performing a live analysis of a computer, one of the first things investigators should collect is the content of RAM. By collecting the contents of RAM first, investigators minimize the impact of their data collection activity on the contents of RAM.

These are some of the specific types of volatile information that investigators should collect:

- system time
- logged-on user (s)
- open files
- network connections
- process information
- process-to-port mapping
- process memory
- network status
- clipboard contents
- service/driver information
- command history
- mapped drives, shares

Tools for Collecting Volatile Information On Windows

To collect volatile information from a Windows system, you could use the following free software tools, which belong to the **Sysinternals** suite provided by Microsoft. You can download it for free from Microsoft's website: http://technet.microsoft.com/en-us/sysinternals/bb842062. After downloading it, you should install it on the root (C:\) of you forensic workstation hard disk. You'll use these commands (unsurprisingly) in the command line interface, like this:

psloggedon

This Sysinternals program enables you to see who is logged on the system locally as well as those users who are logged on remotely.

time /t command

Use this command to see the system actual time. Windows shows file times in UTC which is also GMT (Universal time). The file time is shown down to the 100th nanosecond in a hexadecimal 8 bit format. Windows system time is shown in 32 bit, displaying month, day, year, weekday, hour, minute, second, and millisecond.

net session

This command shows not only the names of the users accessing the system via a remote logon session but also the IP address and the types of clients from which they are accessing the system.

openfiles

This command lists users logged in to a system remotely; investigators should also see what files they have open, if any. This command is used to list or disconnect all files and folders that are open on a system.

psfile

This program also belongs to the Sysinternals suite discussed above. It's a command line program that shows a list of files on a system that are open remotely. It allows a user to close open files either by name or by file identifier.

net file

This command display the names of all open shared files on a system and the number of files locks, and closes individual shared files and removes file locks.

The Microsoft tech web site listed above for Sysinternals explains each tool within the suite and ways the tools can be modified with switches. Overall, this package is a powerful set of utilities for forensic specialists and network technicians.

One last spot you might want to look for deleted files is in the thumbs preview database for windows. Look for a file listed as thumbs.db_. This will show you all the thumbnail images of files viewed in explorer as thumbnails.

Non-volatile Information

Non-volatile information is kept on secondary storage devices and persists after a system is powered down. It's not perishable and can be collected after the volatile information is collected. The following are some of the specific types of non-volatile information that investigators should collect:

- slack space

- hidden files

- swap files

- index.dat files

- meta data

- hidden ADS (Alternate Data Streams)

- Windows Search index

- unallocated clusters

- unused partitions

- registry settings

- connected devices

- event logs

Exercises

Let's play with ADS (Alternate Data Streams) in Windows!

1. Use cmd.exe to start a command prompt.

2. Create a file and put some data in it (I chose to name it ads.txt)

```
C:\>echo This is the primary text. > ads.txt
```

3. Create an alternate data stream in ads.txt (I chose to name it "alt") and put some data in it:

```
C:\>echo This is the alternate text. >  ads.txt:alt
```

4. Find all files and note the ADS is not mentioned:

```
C:\>dir ads*
Volume in drive C has no label.
Volume Serial Number is 42DA-AC49
Directory of C:\
27-10-2016  23:45        28 ads.txt
```

5. Use powershell to find the ADS:

```
PS C:\> get-item -path .\ads.txt -stream *
FileName: C:\Users\root\ads.txt

Stream                      Length
:$DATA                         28
alt.txt                        30
```

6. Use powershell to display the content (in this case):

```
 PS C:\Users\root> get-content -path .\ads.txt -stream ""
```
This is the primary text.
```
 PS C:\Users\root> get-content -path .\ads.txt -stream alt
```
This is the alternate text.

7. To copy an existing file into an ADS:

```
type HHS_en8_Forensics.v2.pdf > ads.txt:pdf
```

8. Read the PDF by starting your favorite PDF-reader and open the file:

```
readpdf ads.txt:pdf
```

eady? Roll Cameras, Action!

Anytime an object (a file) is acted upon by another object (an intruder), there will be residual effects. The effects might not be easy to locate or detect, but those actions (of deleting or modifying) will cause some other results elsewhere. To reduce detectable actions, a professional hacker will use the tools that are already built into the system. They won't introduce new software, instead they will use the system tools in a manner that seems normal.

Windows Server 2008 Event Log editing and location

```
[HKEY_LOCAL_MACHINE\SYSTEM\CurrentControlSet\Services\EventLog
\Application]
```

```
%WinDir%\System32\Winevt\Logs
```

You can also use Windows Powershell to view all of the security logs in one command:

```
get-eventlog security
```

If you want to look at a specific security event, try

```
$events = get-eventlog security -newest 20
```

Exercises

8.16 Even if you aren't using Windows Sever, locate the following logs in windows: Set up, Application, Forwarded Events, and Security. What "number" of events are in each log for your computer? What "type" are each event listed as?

8.17 While we are looking at event logs, let's create a "custom view" so you can see critical events from selected logs. Wow, look at that. Can you import a custom view? Which filters would you select for large events such as "Application" logs?

8.18 Grab a copy of Sysinternals from the web page listed. You will see that this program is a group of smaller programs, very powerful programs. Take a close look at the use of switches for some of the mini programs. Can any of those programs be used together (combined) to create a whole new program?

Linux Forensics

Linux is often used in computer forensics because it:

- Treats every device as file

- Does not need a separate write blocker (forensics requires a hardware write blocker to keep the integrity of the data intact)

- Is highly flexible to work across many operating systems and file types

- Can be booted from removable media

- Is often bundled as a forensic tool kit with multiple tools

    Linux, as with Unix, does not have **alternative datastreams** that are connected to files. The datastreams associated with Linux are not destroyed if you are using most file wiping utilities. To wipe a file securely, the file should not be recoverable since it should be deleted from the media. A proper wiping means that the file could only be recovered at extreme expense or not at all.

    A file removed using the command

    ```
    /bin/rm file_name
    ```

    still remains on the media and can be recovered without much effort.

Linux Slack

Linux file systems do contain slack space, just as Windows does. The slack space is much smaller, roughly 4K per block. This means that a suspect can hide about 4 KB of data in a small file block. The same techniques we discussed in Windows slack space can be applied to Linux slack space. This space is undetectable by filesystem and disk usage tools. When data is removed or deleted, the slack space will remain with the contents of any hidden data.

Silly String

Text strings in Linux are fairly easy to search for and locate using the command

```
/dev/hdaX | grep 'text you want to look for'
```

Depending on the size of the media, this search can take quite a while because it will look for that text everywhere in that partition. You will not want to use a hex editor, since this will take even longer to perform. A hex editor can be useful to determine to contents of that media, though.

Grep

Grep is an immensely powerful Linux tool. It is used to find certain lines within a file. This allows you to quickly find files that contain certain things within a directory or file system. It also allows for searching on regular expressions. There are search patterns that allow you to specify criteria that the search must match. For example: finding all strings in the dictionary that start with "s" and finish with "t" to help with doing a crossword.

```
grep ^s.*t$ /usr/share/dict/words
```

More Command-line Tools

The "Live" forensic tools we discussed earlier are complete Linux forensic toolkits. Linux itself has a number of simple utilities for imaging and basic disk analysis, including the following:

Tool	Description
dd	The dd command can copy data from from any disk that Linux can mount and access.
	This command can make a bit-stream disk-to-disk file, disk-to-image file, block-to-block copy/block-to-file copy.
sfdisk and fdisk	Displays the disk structure.
grep	Searches files for instances of an expression or pattern.
md5sum and sha1sum	Creates and stores an MD5 or SHA-1 hash of a file or list of files (including devices).

file	Reads file header information to tell its type, regardless of name or extension.
xxd	A command-line hex dump tool
ghex and khexedit	Gnome and KDE (X windows interface) hex editors

Finding a Haystack in a Needle

Open Source forensic software includes powerful search tools that let you search for many combinations and permutations of factors for deep data searching. There is no need to buy expensive commercial tools, which is the wonderful part of using Open Source software. Linux provides you with plenty of scope to construct similar tools using standard utilities. The following text details the use of find, grep and strings, and then describes the use of the pipe to combine them.

Encryption, Decryption and File Formats

Many of the files that you will come across will not be immediately readable. Most programs have their own proprietary file formats, while others use standard formats – for example the standard picture formats - gif, jpg, png, etc. Linux provides an excellent utility to help you to determine what a given file is. Remember the **file** command from above?

Command Line Switch	Effect
-k	Don't stop at the first match, keep going
-L	Follow symbolic links
-z	Attempt to look inside compressed files

hese switches let you try to read a file. There are a number of file conversion utilities available to you under Linux, and even more available on the Internet, as well as a number of file viewers for various formats. Sometimes it may require more than one step to get to a place where you can really work with the data – try to think laterally!

Occasionally, you will come across files which have been encrypted or password protected. The complication that this presents varies, from encryption that is easily broken to stuff that would even give the best decryption professionals a headache. It pays to examine the area surrounding the computer that you are dealing with. People aren't very good at remembering passwords; they may well be written down somewhere nearby. Common choices for passwords also involve: pets, relatives, dates (marriage, date of birth), telephone numbers, car registrations, and other simple combinations (123456, abcdef, qwerty etc.). People are also reluctant to use more than one or two passwords for everything, so if you can reverse engineer a password on one file or application, try it on the others. It is highly likely to be the same. Take a look at Lesson 11 Passwords for more information on cracking passwords.

Exercises

8.19   Boot up with Linux and create a file named "evil plans" on a USB drive or any other portable rewritable media.

8.20   Delete that file using whatever technique you wish.

8.21   Hand that media to your lab partner and tell them you lost a file. Ask them to recover the lost file but don't tell your partner the name of the file you "lost."

8.22   Try this recovery process with other types of media and operating systems, changing out with your lab partner.

8.23   How many times does it take to format a drive or removable media to ensure that all previous data or a single file is erased?

8.24   If a partition is removed and reallocated, is the previous data lost forever or can it be recovered? What tools would you use to attempt such a task?

8.25   Hide a secret file in the slack space of another file. Delete the main file. Can the hidden data be recovered and how would you do it if it is possible at all?

8.26   If the encryption method is too strong to be broken, it may be necessary to perform a dictionary attack (also called a brute force attack). Find out what a dictionary attack is.

8.27   Find out what Truecrypt is and how it works. Learn about hidden containers. Do you think you would be able to access such an archive? How? (One answer: http://xkcd.com/538/)

Feed Your Head: Real Case Studies

Here are some examples to show digital forensics at work.

Who	What
Morgan Stanley	In a Florida court case, Morgan Stanley (MS) repeatedly failed to turn over data related to a fraud suit against them. 1423 backup tapes were concealed by MS that contained emails detailing the fraud. A fired MS technician revealed to the court that those tapes existed and many other tapes were deliberately mislabeled. Forensic examination confirmed this intentional fraud. The judge fined MS $1.6 billion dollars for acting with "malice or evil" intent.
David Kernell	In September 2008, the defendant hacked into Sarah Palin's Yahoo email account. Before the FBI arrived to investigate this crime, Kernell uninstalled his web browser and fragmented his hard drive. The government was able to provide sufficient forensic and testimonial evidence of his crime to convict him on a number of counts.
TJX A.K.A. Albert Gonzalez	One of the longest convictions ever handed down for a computer crime was given to TJX. Gonzalez was convicted of stealing 90 million credit card and debit card numbers. The defendant ran a gang of cyber-thieves over several years and bought a yacht for himself using the stolen money. Teams of digital forensic examiners were called in to crack the case and provide evidence. TJX was issued a 20 year prison sentence and ordered to pay $25,000.

Mobile Forensics

Using mobile communications as a tool in your planning and/or execution of the hack can provide you with a completely new set of options. Cell phones use several forms of signaling, one is the radio that links your phone to the closest antenna receiver, the next is the Bluetooth link that works for short-range connections, the GPS signal locator can be used for other functions, and lastly the phone has digital connection capabilities. We want to focus on the digital portion of a cellphone.

Inside a cell phone is a Subscriber Identification Module (SIM) card that identifies your phone to you and your service provider. This SIM card is also the same card that stores some of your phone numbers and other text data. This card has an onboard microprocessor.

SIM cards contain a special set of numbers known as International Mobile Subscriber Identity (IMSI). The IMSI is the phone number for that device and can be thought of as a Machine Access Code (MAC) address for a cellular phone. The first set of numbers of a MDN are assigned to the manufacture. SIM card editors like the ones available at Dekart will assist you in viewing this number set.

If you were going to conduct special business on a cell phone that might be traced, it is quite possible to have several SIM cards on hand. Changing out the cards after each call makes it nearly impossible to trace a cellular call. International SIM cards with preloaded calling credits are available in Europe, Korea, Japan, and other countries that do not have a cellular monopoly as in the United States.

One point to consider is that cellular devices are tracked from cellular tower to tower, even if the device is just on. This is part of the normal communication hand-off to ensure the cellular caller can make a connection quickly, at any time. In the near future, towers will track and maintain logs of each cellular device that pass through their zones while communicating. This may sound contradictory to the paragraph above, however, the SIM card contains the hand-set identifier. Changing out SIM chips is almost like changing out cellular devices.

Short Message Service (SMS) are stored by each cellular phone carrier for several days or none at all. This shows how quickly evidence can disappear and timely response is critical. The messages are saved on the user's phone, usually on the SIM card or on the external memory card.

So how do you feel about the track-ability of YOUR phone?

Connect the Blue Wire to the Red Square

Another aspect of cellular digital communications is the ability to use Voice Over Internet Protocol (VOIP). This communication tool uses VOIP software to create data voice communications between you and another VOIP user, bypassing cell phone usage charges. Wonderful, right? How could this possibly help you?

Well, since VOIP is digital and a piece of software, we can encrypt the packets if you are using the Android OS. The Advanced Encryption Standard (AES) is a block cipher and can provide many levels of security. You will want to use the lowest encryption level, since VOIP is already going to be slow over a data phone.

Some Disassembly Required

Before you attempt to recover any data from a cellphone, turn off the cellular signal, as in put the phone in "Airplane" mode. Cellular providers can disable or delete all data from a device if that device is reported as lost or stolen. Don't be that one person who forgets to disable the signal to the mother ship.

Older devices used proprietary cabled for charging and transferring data. These cables changed from device to device and never seemed to be interchangeable to anything. These days, most devices connect using a mini USB cable on one end and a standard USB on the other. Apple products are the exception to this standard for "security" reasons.

As secure as this sounds, the Apple to computer interface cable ends as a USB connection at one end. If that doesn't seems to work well enough, you can purchase the pad Camera adapter kit. The kit includes a straight USB link to the pad plus another adapter that connects a SD card directly to the Pad. So this gives you the option of plugging a SD card or a USB drive directly into the Pad. Cool, huh?

Cellular devices can store data in any one of three local areas. These areas are: The phone's built-in memory, the SIM card, and the external memory card. The good stuff (real evidence) is often located on the phone's internal memory and on the SIM card. SMS enabled devices often include software for "predictive text." Predictive text files can include portions or entire text messages that may not be located elsewhere.

So Many Devices, So Little Time

Way back when, phones just called out and received voice transmissions. These things were connected to a wall, a deck, or payphone booth. These days phones are no longer just phones, they are portable networked computers. Cellular communications comes in all different sizes and models. An iPad isn't a phone but it can communicate in many of the same ways a cellphone can. A tablet, Android OS, Pocket PCs, all have many of the same features as a phone but cannot be called a phone at all. "Dude, let me borrow your tablet so I can call my friend," is something you're not going to hear just yet, but you will. Then you'll have to worry they're going to find your love letters, or your porn, or put love letters or porn on your phone.

Products that run on the Android OS are fairly straightforward to exam due to Google's open operating system. Android is based on the Linux kernel, which was covered earlier. Google provides its Android source code and a developer's tool kit free of charge. Other device OSs include Black Berry, Windows, Windows CE, Nokia, Symbian, and Linux.

Each OS will need to store files in some order and there are not too many different ways to name "SMS" or "Video" files. A little snooping around on each different device using the software listed below should give you the evidence you are looking for (which is, by the way, why you shouldn't fee invulnerable, or even "protected," on your device).

Besides the fact that cellular devices have Bluetooth, data transmission, and WiFI communication capabilities, many are GPS enabled as well. All of these signals store information on the phone, the SIM card or on the external memory card. Forensic software allows an examination of each type of history, including the GPS. If the suspect enabled their GPS, all the waypoints and location history can be recovered to provide even more evidence. http://www.gpsvisualizer.com/ allows you to upload GPS data and will create maps to show you where that where that data leads.

Don't forget about the suspect's vehicle GPS as well as the on-board computer. Any vehicle built over the past 3 decades (since 1985 in the U.S.) has a diagnostic computer that tracks speed, fuel consumption, ignition sequence, plus more information that may help you solve the case. Expect shoes to start keeping track of your location. You might even be able to make phone calls with them too.

iDevices: There are some folks have dedicated time and effort into open source projects such as IPBackup Analyzer. The purpose of this program is to look at data that is backed up on an iPhone and make it readable. You can find this open source software at http://ipbackupanalyzer.com/. One of the unique issues with Apple mobile products is the requirement for a back-up passcode. The passcode can be bypassed using software tools, which will allow for examination of text messages, phone contacts, pictures, video, emails and all evidence you might need to examine.

iPhone Forensics Example

Check out this article on an iPhone forensic investigation:
http://www.nxtbook.com/nxtbooks/evidencetechnology/20120910/#/30

Warning -This article deals with a sensitive topic that you may find offensive.

Phone Software Tools

Most of the major phone forensic software builders have found a niche market that allows them to charge a premium for their tools. There are a few open source and free products out there you might want to look into. Like anything else, each tool has pro's and con's but, you will need to have a working knowledge of several tools to be successful.

Oxygen: This software and hardware manufacture offers several types of cellular forensic products. This software is free for limited time use, roughly six months. If you can't get the data you want out of a device in six months, you might want to try the "Hammer" method. You can download the free version of Oxygen Forensic Suite 2012 at http://www.oxygen-forensic.com/en/freeware/. This software is capable of reading iPhone back ups, even if the data is protected by iTunes passwords. Nice.

Bit Pim: An open source project, Bit Pim has been used for a number of years. This free software has one tiny drawback, the lack of support for newer smart phones. To be honest, Bit Pim doesn't work on quite a few newer smart phones. Luckily for you, the authors will try and create a package for you if you ask them nicely. Actually, you have to follow their rules listed in the Web site under "FYI", if you want any response from them. Failure to adhere to their request process will result in nothing. You will get nothing from them, period. Read their documentation at http://www.bitpim.org/.

Sleuth Kit: We talked at Sleuth Kit earlier in this lesson. Another open source program with tons of features, including cellular forensics, Sleuth Kit gives you the same capabilities as many commercial products. You can find more than enough information about the product including an entire Wiki at www.sleuthkit.org.

https://viaforensics.com/products/tools/ offers several free links to Android OS forensic tools. This site offers a book on Android Forensincs plus several scripts for gathering your own data. These folks are also the one who have a section dedicated to iPhone forensics at https://viaforensics.com. Remember, an apple a day, keeps the iTunes back-up away.

Now What?

If a digital device is evidence in a case, do not turn off the device if at all possible. Find a battery charger, get a charger, or build a charger if you have to but keep that device running if it is already turned on. This is critical if the phone is a pay-as-you-go since there isn't a signed contract with a mobile carrier. These phones are difficult to trace because they are disposable.

Of course you can't examine nor copy the SIM data without removing the battery. This is another reason to keep the cellular device powered by another way without relying on the battery. With our luck, the device battery will always be just about dead anyways. Bad guys never remember to charge of their devices.

The forensic examination should be done using direct cables from the device to your awesome lab computer. This means that all other communication means need to be shut off. Bluetooth, WiFi, GPS, and whatever else has to be turned off before an examination can begin. Failure to do so could render the evidence useless in a court of law.

Exercises

8.28 Grab a Mini USB cable and connect a cellular device to your computer. The device should ask you one question with three possible answers. What are those three answers? Which one should you choose if you want to evaluate the data on your device?

Once you have a link between your computer and the target device, look to see what information you can obtain on your own. How far could you get without any special software? Could you read any data on the device itself or just what is on the external memory card?

Disconnect the link and download any cellular forensic software that you like onto your computer. Install the software. Turn your target device off, then on again. Now reestablish that cable connection you had from the first question. Okay, now you can run the new forensic software you downloaded. Can you access all of the SIM data or just parts of it?

Do not touch your PUK or Pin!! Most phones will lock-up if the PUK or Pin is guessed too many times. What is the PUK or Pin and why it is critical to you as an examiner?

8.29   Steal someone's cell, ha, ha, just kidding. Borrow someone's cellphone and connect it to your high-speed Cray Supercomputer. Can you access their SMSs, photos, contacts, caller log? What is the serial number of that phone; the one that is hard coded into the SIM, not the one on the inside of the case?

Network Forensics

Network forensics are used to find out where a computer is located and to prove whether a particular file was sent from a particular computer over a network. While network forensics can be very complicated, we will cover some of the basics that can be applied to everyday life, and how you can find things out – or be found out.

Firewall Logs

Who's connecting to you? The firewall is a utility that can control connections between two points in a network. There are many types of firewalls. Regardless of the firewall type and job of the firewall, it is the firewall logs, which give you the details. By using the logs you can find patterns of attacks and abuse to your firewall.

As with any log file, the integrity of those files are essential. Think of log files as a **smoking gun**. Each file is stamped with time/date and certain property rights. Firewall logs are considered "smart" logs because they are generated from a device that has perimeters and is not a simple hub or switch box. Each packet is not recorded but each request and connection is recorded. You are looking for connections between specific IP addresses or the transmission of files between two connections.

Packet Sniffers

Packets of data flow through the veins of every networked device. Since there are literally millions of packets moving between servers and other devices, looking at individual packets had always been thought to be impossible. With the increased power of computers and better software technology, we now have the capabilities to search through millions of transmitted packets to locate those that meet our requirements. We call this technique "packet sniffing."

Imagine that you are on a bus loaded with people. Everyone is talking but you want to hear just one conversation from two seats away. Your brain has the ability to tune out other noise and focus on that one conversation. Packet sniffing does the same thing; it filters out all the other noise and concentrates on the packets you are interested in.

Packet sniffers come in all kinds of shapes and sizes but every type must be placed between the data flow transmissions. You can't hear a conversation if you are not with the people who are talking. Packet sniffers can be active (looking) or passive (listening) yet, either type will gather packets that match your requests. The trick for an intruder is how to gather, store, and transmit those packets in your network without getting caught.

Intrusion Detection Systems (IDS)

This tempting name is a generic term for anything that can detect, alert, or shut down abnormal network activities. Snort is a perfect example of a program that can look for abnormal behavior in network traffic. An example of odd behavior would be if you were on vacation and your email account became active. Your account started to send and receive all types of attachments and redirected emails, as though someone were using your email account. An IDS would pick up on this weird behavior and either act on its own to shut off the account or notify someone that some strange stuff is going on while you are away.

IDS were designed to be the watchdog of network traffic. Each type of IDS looks for protocols, signatures, ports and other locations where odd behavior might happen. Some systems deny all and only allow authenticated users through, while other IDS's bait and wait. The IDS's logs are full of wonderful details on odd behavior.

Router and Network Management Logs

As mentioned in the firewall logs, routers and network management logs are very detailed in their collection of typical activities. Occasionally something will pop up in the logs that will trigger a forensic expert's interest on a case. Besides being evidence to prove when certain events occurred, log files are difficult to tamper with. The software tools we have mentioned before have programs to automate log filtering. Using automation tools will save you both time and sanity in the long run.

Tools of the Network Trade

There are a variety of open source software tools that should be part of any network evidence collectors kit, starting with the tried and true **Wireshark**. Since network traffic is data packets, or chunks of information, Wireshark captures and analyzes packets. Instead of making you going line by line through each packet to identify headers, routing information, sender, and the contents of each packet, Wireshark does all the heavy lifting for you. Plus, Wireshark is a cross platform utility.

Netcat at http://netcat.sourceforge.net/ is another powerful open source program that analyzes all network traffic including TCP and UDP, inbound and outbound, Ethernet and IP, including any service or port you'd like to look at. Like Wireshark, Netcat is a cross platform application. Both are actively updated by a team of volunteers.

Netcat has a **hexdump** utility built into the software and can capture/analyze packets.

E-Mail Headers

E-mails come with information of every computer they pass through to get to you. This is added to the **header** portion of the email information. Sometimes the most important information is in the headers. To view the headers, however, is not always so simple. Various mail clients will all have different ways to view this. The real trick to reading headers, though, is to know they are read backwards. The top of the list is the receiver. Each route the email travels goes with each line until the very last line is the computer or network that the mail was sent from.

This is only true if the email sender used their real email address to send it. Emails can be spoofed, IP addressed can be faked, and all sorts of other tricks might be used to disguise the real sender. The header can provide some clues but don't expect to solve any cases based just on email header information.

Within the email header, there is segment called "Message-ID." This set of characters is provided by the first email server when the message was sent. Since each ID is unique, proper logging can help you identify the location of the original sender. Look for the link listed right after the series of numbers and letter in the ID.

The sender "From" information in the header is configured by the email client and should not be considered reliable. Time stamps can also be misleading because email clients can be configured to send emails hours or days after the email was written. This is a technique known as "Delayed Send."

Exercises

8.30   Grab any Spam email you have in your email box. Using the information provided, dissect the email header in an attempt to locate the source of that spam. How did that spammer get your email address?

8.31   Determine how to look at your e-mail headers in the e-mails you receive. Are there any particular fields in those headers that seem foreign to you? You probably have several email accounts. Forge yourself an email, try your best to hide your actual location.

8.32   Send that spoofed/forged email to your lab partner telling them that they need to pick up something, like donuts, for the next class. Make sure the spoofed sender is the instructor, otherwise you might not get your donuts.

8.33   If you have a social media email address, send yourself an email from that social media site to your regular email account. Take a look at the social media email header to see if you can tell how that email was routed.

8.34   Now, try that same exercise again but send the social media email as an anonymous to you regular account. Check the anonymous email header to see if you can tell how well your identification is hidden by the social media service.

Game On: Getting Down and Dirty

"Please tell me what you are doing in the school dumpster," Mokoa asked, scratching his windblown hair. Two legs dangled against the lip of the large green trash bin while the other half of Jace grappled with bags of garbage in the container.

"Just hold the lid open for me," yelled the trash intruder. The side of the metal bin released a loud "clunk" as something large struck the inside. "I got it! Now pull me up," Jace yelled in Mokoa's general direction. The echo of her voice in the trash bin sounded as if she were talking through a soup can with a rubber balloon stuffed inside. The thought of soup made her nauseas as she clung onto the prize junk she dug out of the dumpster.

Mokoa grabbed the two legs, trying hard to avoid being kicked in the face and pivoted the smelly hacker up and over the trash dumpster's opening. To both of their surprise, Jace popped up out of the trash bin holding a used mobile tablet in her arms and she didn't even drop it, yet. With her shoes planted softly back on the parking lot asphalt, she held the battered slim case as a trophy for her dirty work.

"Check it out, this is the old teacher's lounge time card device," Jace beamed with glory. As any lady would do, she brushed back her tattered hair so she would look her best in this moment of triumph. In that brief second, the slippery case slid out of the single hand and landed nicely on top of her foot.

Mokoa had never heard Jace cuss that much before and he certainly had never seen her howl in pain that loud. He did his best to avoid enjoying his best friend in pain, mainly because he was usually the one who suffered the injuries when they were together.

Mokoa put his hands on his hips and lectured to the injured girl, "I haven't heard that much cussing since the last time I went to church!"

Jace forgot all about her wounded toes as she looked with strange eyes at her friend, "What are you talking about? You're weird dude."

He dropped his arms down and explained, "At church they're always talking about hell and us being "damned" and stuff like that." Mokoa was trying to lighten up the mood, to cheer up Jace even though his humor was awful.

"Mokoa, that joke was more painful than my foot right now," jabbed Jace. "But check out the other cool gadget I found in the trash," she said as she pulled out a smashed cellphone from her hip pocket.

With a tone of pure boredom Mokoa responded with, "Wow, a wrecked cellphone to go along with a destroyed tablet. What are you going to do with all this wonderful treasure?"

Jace twisted her head slightly as her mouth formed a grin reserved for evil geniuses. "Just wait," she said.

Back at the lab, well, more like back at Jace's small bedroom in the apartment she shared with her grandmother, Jace had the back covers pulled off the devices. Even after she had wiped down the devices the stench was still lingering in the poorly ventilated room.

"So, what are we looking at," Mokoa asked as he peered over Jace's slim shoulder at the pair of broken gadgets. He backed off a step as soon as he realized that she smelled just as bad as the trash dumpster.

"First of all, I need to find out what operating system these things use," she replied without looking at Mokoa.

"But you can figure that out just by looking at the case. That one runs IMO because it was built by Anvil and has the Anvil stamp right on it and that smaller one runs Robot. It says right on the back of the thing."

"Dude, just because it was built and packaged by a brand doesn't mean it runs that operating system. You can root the devices and replace whatever OS you want, plus you can add modifications to the internal chips using EPROMs to dual boot. And don't get me started when it comes to fake phones made in Hinad. You never know what is on those things."

Mokoa took another step back and said, "Okay, I'll step back and shut up now."

"No you won't. You can't be quiet any more than I can. I'll walk you through the steps I take to gather data. Grab a seat," Jace said knowing that the only chair around was in the kitchen.

"Oh, and while you're getting a chair grab me some cookies and a tall glass of ice water."

Mokoa knew the drill since Jace was an expert at getting him to do chores for her.

It took him three trips to the kitchen and back to get the cookies, water, chair, and a snack for himself. He finally sat down behind Jace as she began her tutorial.

"80% of these mobile devices run different flavors of two OS's, Robot and Anvil. Robot has a million versions of it, with each version slightly different based on who manufactured it. IMO was written by one single company so there isn't much variation in those mobile devices. Robot is much easier to image then IMO, since IMO is a closed OS and is very tight on security access. If this device is running IMO but it was jailbroken, I'll have an easier time obtaining the encrypted pin."

Mokoa understand most of what Jace was saying but knew not to disturb her while she worked. He could ask questions when she stopped to drink water or bite into a cookie. Otherwise, he kept quiet and watched her work.

Jace continued, "Each OS stores data differently. Luckily, Robot was written based on the Linux kernel and Software Developer Kits (SDK) are easy to download from the creators of Robot. This is fairly open-source software. IMO isn't. If the mobile phone or tablet has IMO and the user employed a PIN to lock the machine, our work is much tougher. It's not impossible to recover the data; it just means more work for me."

A laptop was pulled out from inside Jace's knapsack; again, Mokoa was given the task of fetching the computer for Jace. She flipped open the portable computer and had the programs running while she hunted for USB cables in her desk drawer. While she rummaged for cables, Mokoa reached over and pressed buttons on each of the trashed machines. None of the buttons seemed to work.

"Hey genius," Jace shot out, "I already tried that. I wouldn't be digging for connection cables if the things powered up."

Mokoa felt a bit stupid as usual. Jace never missed small details like trying to power up a machine first.

"Yes! I found the two I need. I hope they work," Jace said as she untangled a mess of wires.

"Um, Jace, had you thought about taking a shower before we keep going? You really smell bad, like Mr. Tri bad," Mokoa couldn't bear the stench any longer.

"BAD! You think I as smell as bad as Mr. Tri! I'll show you bad," She steamed and back handed Mokoa faster than he ever expected since he was sitting behind her.

"What was that for? You stink and I can't stand sitting next to you. I'm leaving until you shower and apologize for that smack," Mokoa said as he was walking out of Jace's room. The apartment door slammed shut.

Upset by the whole situation, she smelled her hair and really felt bad for what she did to her friend. Jace cussed to herself.

Game Over

Let the Fun Begin

A critical part of a hack is thinking through the entire process before touching the keyboard.

- How are you going to get inside your target?

- What controls do you need to disable or monitor during your network visit?

- What do you want and where is the location of your target?

- How are you going to transfer the data you want and where are you going to store it?

- What logs and audits need to be restarted or edited as you exit to cover your tracks?

- Where are you planning to keep the new data for your safety and use?

Social engineering is an excellent tool for gaining access to physical locations and networks. Recognizing it is a great way to be immune to (some or most of) it.

Reconnaissance

Recon is learning the networks vulnerabilities, the types of servers you will be dealing with. What security measures are being used and what are their vulnerabilities. Can you turn those security devices to your advantage? Where are the network logs and audit logs kept? Are you going to install a backdoor for return work? What attack vectors are you comfortable using and will work across each network?

Software and hardware vulnerabilities

You can locate all known exploits and vulnerabilities on all types of products by going to http://www.cvedetails.com/ or www.cve.mitre.org/. Both of these web sites should be part of your attack methodology as soon as you learn anything about the networks you will be dealing with.

OpenVAS

OpenVAS at http://www.openvas.org/ is an open source vulnerability scanner and manager. The organizations own **Network Vulnerability Test (NVT)** database is used to update the scanner on a daily basis. This "One-stop-shopping" for vulnerabilities can be compared with CVE, without all the extra technical jargon. The software is a collection of tools that you can shape to fit your needs, even if you just want to know which vulnerabilities apply to an Apache web server.

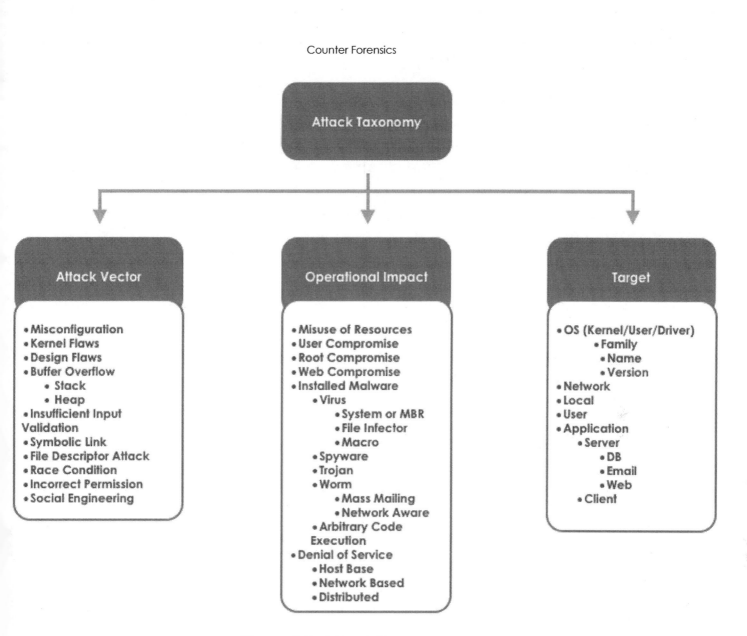

Figure 8.3: Attack Taxonomy

Attack Vectors: These are methods to enter networks, using a variety of tools or known vulnerabilities. You will often see this term used alongside "malware," since attack vectors are mainly viewed as malicious network entry points by the security professionals. In our use of the term, we are merely showing you the types of ways to enter networks, in a specific category. Repeat after me, "I will not use Attack Vectors to plant malware." Hold your hand in an official looking manner when you say that, too, so it sounds like a pledge or something. Because this stuff can land you in jail, and we don't want to be the people who catch you. We'll leave that for your friends.

Weapons to Hack Networks

Blackhole is a package of "mouse click" exploits aimed at giving any hacker with any degree of skill, several ways to gain administrator access on a network. Unlike most other exploit software; Blackhole 1.0 earned a name for itself in the security industry because the program introduced several zero-day vulnerabilities. The creators of version 2.0 are promising "dynamic URL's" provided by another AV company, which would effectively build custom exploits just for you.

http://malware.dontneedcoffee.com/2012/09/blackhole2.0.html Cost is $50 for one day of use. Such a deal!

THC-Hydra 7.3 was updated in May 2012 and Hydra works to crack network logon passwords. The program has an excellent use for switches in the command prompt for Linux. This program can be run through a proxy (to hide your location), through FTP, IRC, HTTP, and several other protocols.

http://www.thc.org/thc-hydra/

Metasploit has been around as a penetration testing software in the open source community. There are now several commercial flavors of Metasploit, with the one you want being free. Like many community based tools, Metasploit has a large library of add-ons, plug-in, and configurations. Many security professionals have this software as part of their "have to have" toolbox. You will want it because there are additional exploits added all the time to the Metasploit engine.

http://www.metasploit.com/

The **Fedora Security Spin** is another community project aimed at education and the safe testing of security tools. Fedora Linux is really customizable: you can create your own **spin** with exactly the apps you want, and nothing you don't want. The Security Spin is all about security testing and auditing, which sounds kind of formal but actually is really fun. Like many security tools, the package is distributed in an ISO format that can be put on a USB thumb drive or CD. And like Fedora itself, the vast majority of professionally built security software is open source.

Cain and Able is the ultimate in Script Kiddie software. Cain was originally designed as a standalone program to recover passwords from SAM dumps (Windows password files). The program is still excellent at performing that same task, just finding anyone running an old version of Windows is difficult. Able was added to increase the usefulness of the tool and build a penetration-testing package. Cain and Able together offer really easy access to really insecure networks.

http://www.oxid.it/cain.html

Fyodor boasts 125 Top Security Network Security Tools. This list has been available for a number of years and is updated (sort of). Not only does the web site provide you a brief description of each tool but it also provides you a like to the software. Some of the tools are quite old but useful when working with FORTRAN or an abacus. Check the site regularly, at least every few years, for new tools that you have already heard of.

http://sectools.org/

Exercises

8.35   Head over to Metasploit.com and download the most recent copy. Burn the ISO onto either a bootable USB device or a "live" DVD."

The kind folks at Metasploit provide a vulnerable server that allows you to work with the tools in Metasploit without getting into legal trouble. The server is called "Metasploitable." Create an account, get Metasploitable and try out your new pentesting software.

Game On: Making Up for a Big Stink

Jace spent three days trying to get the nasty trash dumpster smell off her and three more days trying to apologize to Mokoa. She felt lonely without having him around, even after he made Jace promise to never touch his face again. Jace's heart sunk slightly, ever so slightly at the thought of losing her best friend and having to be cautious when she was around him. She has always taken their friendship for granted since they were always around each other. For six days she was alone and she didn't like the feeling of being without Mokoa. This cruel absence changed the way she thought about him.

Mokoa finally agreed to meet Jace back at her apartment to continue the mobile devices investigations. He felt a bit uneasy around Jace; she was acting differently like he was something new to her. She was nicer and spoke in a softer tone to him. She even looked him in the eyes when they talked. Jace never did that before. He wasn't sure how to take this new personality of hers but he liked the gentler side anyways.

Back at the lab, Jace positioned her chair so Mokoa had a decent view of what she was doing on her bedroom desk. She had cookies and milk already arranged on the desk for them to share. Mokoa eyed the strange actions and was wondering what the hell was going on with her.

Jace turned to face Mokoa, which surprised him, since he usually sees the backside of her head when she is working on computers. She started, "Remember the two mobile devices we got out of the school dumpster last week?"

Mokoa nodded with suspicion. He squinted his leather brown eyes as he surveyed her tiny room for booby traps or a hidden video camera. "There has to be some prank going on," he thought. "What is she up to?" She continued the conversation only when he rejoined eye contact with her.

"First we have a cellphone that has been damaged and the SIM card was removed before it was tossed in the trash. I cleaned it up so it doesn't smell like before."

Mokoa hadn't noticed the fresh smell of her room until she mentioned the cellphone being clean. Her room appeared different, more feminine. It smelled and looked like someone else lived there because Jace never kept her room that clean before. Jasmine and a hint of pine oil floated in the air near Mokoa. It was a nice change of pace from the foot locker odor that had always filled her room. "Where's the hidden camera," he thought to himself.

She repositioned herself, actually correcting her normally bad posture. With her back straight in the desk chair and the two devices in front of her, she began her lecture.

"There are two types of approaches for this challenge. We can either try to gather evidence about a crime or we can mess around the see what we can get out of these things. If we are trying to hack and get data from the phone, we don't really care if we damage it more. But, if we were doing a forensic examination to obtain legal evidence of a crime, then we have a bunch of check-list steps to go through."

Mokoa frowned at the idea of going through a slow and painful list of precise steps. Jace noticed his dismay and said, "Don't worry; I'll just talk about some of the forensic methods. Today, we're interested in seeing what sort of data was left on each device."

"Don't let the phone or tablet connect to any network before you start. Use anything you can think of to keep that device from connecting to a cellular tower or WiFi network. This includes using aluminum foil, lead containers, Faraday cages and metal boxes that can block a radio signal. Cellphones will increase their signal strength in attempts to connect to a carrier."

Mokoa tried to add something intelligent to the conversation, to show that he was paying attention, "What about just turning on Airplane mode."

"Oh wait. Stop, stop, stop," Jace abruptly jumped up out of her seat. She reached into her pant pocket and pulled out her own cellphone with the skull and crossbones sticker on the back.

Mokoa knew this was the prank part of the conversation. He said, "What, what's up? Why all the stop, stop, stop stuff?"

Jace didn't bother to look at Mokoa as she pressed phone buttons to shut down her cell phone. "Dude, before we start, we gotta shut off our phones and anything that might have a connection signal like Bluetooth, WiFi, or whatever. We can't let the devices connect to anything around us." Mokoa shut his phone down too.

"If we use the Airplane mode to stop the device from connecting to a carrier, we'll need to work quickly because most devices can be wiped remotely as soon they connect to a tower."

"Yeah and the internal phone memory is limited, which sorta means that without a SIM card installed, the phone will only remember the last few phone calls it received. A smart criminal trying to hide phone call data will try to call that phone dozens of times hoping to overwrite that limited phone log."

"If we were going to need a forensic image of a SIM card, we'd copy the SIM card before turning on device. When the device is turned on, dozens of applications start running and data in the phone is updated constantly. This spoils any evidence we might be trying to gather if that data is required for like legal purposes. Of course, that's the last thing on my mind. I don't want the law anywhere near me as I do this stuff. I just want the data because I'm curious and nosey."

"iPads can be imaged using the Camera Connection Kit, which allows me to take advantage of the USB Mass Storage Device protocol. As long as the USB drive I'm using has a directory called "/DCIM", the iPad should mount and read the attached drive. iPads can mount and read FAT and HFS partitions using the Picture Transfer Protocol (PTP) as the communication link. iPods and iPhone can be accessed using the USB interface cable. User data is stored on the section partition of the solid state drive in the /private/var directory."

"The funny thing about most of the commercial forensic software programs is that they take advantage of little known exploits or vulnerabilities in that OS. As soon as the cellphone manufacture plugs that hole, your expensive software is worthless until it's updated."

"Oh Dude, don't think for a second that cops don't have access to tools and software to exam this stuff too. The mobile manufactures AND Telephone Companies AND ISP's all keep records of your data and give that information to the police. If the organizations don't have the data, the companies offer the tools to get that personal information off the gadgets they sell."

Mokoa wanted Jace to take a breath for a moment; he could see her face going blue from all the talking. "So what are you trying to tell me, all the privacy we think we have is fake or can be broken if you have a subpoena?"

Jace sucked in air as her eye grew wide, "Dude, you don't even need a subpoena."

Mokoa recognized that this conversation was going to be a huge lecture on privacy rights. Those lectures tended to be exhaustive and involve 100% of his attention as Jace were talking, otherwise she would repeat herself to make sure he got her every word. This was going to be a long, long day.

Game Over

Counter Forensics Software

Counter forensic software tries to perform one or both functions of deleting all log file and/or erasing all data that could have been altered during a network visit. Both method could ring very loud alarms if not used correctly, bringing in the eighty-five agents tha have not had their morning coffee yet. Counter forensic tools are mainly used on a single computer to remove, hide, cover-up, and generally make a forensic examiners job difficult or impossible.

There are a few issues that need to be considered if you plan on using counter forensic software. The first issue is the examiners determination that counter forensic software was actually used on your machine. This alone would raise suspicion as to why anyone would use this software if they didn't have anything to hide.

Second, locating and deleting every bit of data remnants from swap files, temp directories, pagefiles, and every speck of data that could link you to the hack.

Third, forensic examiners are paid either by salary or by the hour. They are primarily paid to produce enough evidence to convict someone. If you have created an evidence recovery challenge that would take too long for any examiner to make a case against you, they will likely stop looking at some point. Time is money. Take your time to add more work for an examiner ahead of time, this time and every time, unless you want to spend time doing hard time for a long time.

Just Who Has the Advantage

There are several opportunities for a criminal to use counter-forensic methods on a device. These include:

- Many forensic examiners do not know how to deal with advanced users who can manipulate the operating system or hide data. The push for new digital forensic personnel has created a "shake n bake" process where the person attends a few classes and is handed a piece of software to use. This leaves so much experience needed to the will of the software manufactures.
- Forensic software doesn't have a set standard for the scientific process of collecting, analyzing, and reporting a repeatable method. Different software will show different results. Thus, results cannot be replicated. This is bad, very bad.
- There is no common body of knowledge amongst digital forensic experts. This means there are several ways to slice an apple, none are right or wrong. There is no established method to conduct a digital forensic examination or even publish the results.
- Digital forensic examiners and software/hardware hasn't been designed for field environments. This stuff was created to be used in a nice clean lab, with perfect conditions, and all the tools you would ever need. In the real world, this is never the case.

- A simple alteration to the evidence, such as a delayed file update or system time change would render the entire forensic collection useless. The data would not be accepted by a court of law because of a simple change.

You Gotta Be Social

Facebook, Twitter, Google, Tumblr and all those social media sites are part of cloud storage. Each of these services offer easy access to users to communicate with friends, meet others, share ideas, post pictures, post their calendars, and socialize in a digital environment. Many of these cloud providers seem to give away their web products without any regard for their own profit. It all appears to be "free."

The concept is simple: provide an online place where people can interact and give them ways to express themselves in an environment that the user thinks is private. As more users join that cloud playground, collect information on each user to create precise marketing materiel for that user. The cloud service can then sell that targeted marketing information to advertisers or product manufactures directly. You could say that it is a "win-win" because users get a nice place to socialize and cloud services can earn enough to stay in business.

Of course, that isn't all the ways these social media providers earn money. Facebook recently announced it had 1 billion users. With that many people across the globe accessing Facebook, that site has become the world's largest personal photo and identification database ever created. Everything that is posted on any of these social sites becomes property of that service. All that personal information is worth a tremendous amount of money.

Think of social media this way; if you are not being sold anything, than you are being sold to someone else. You are the product.

Head in the Clouds

Current forensic laws, tools, and techniques do not work in a cloud setting. Because of the design in cloud computing, any forensic analysis will involve shared resources. What this means is when a forensic examiner attempts to retrieve suspected evidence, they are going to also grab data that belongs to other people, as well. This doesn't mean that an attack against one cloud service is going to go unreported or not investigated. The cloud provider will conduct their own investigation and look at legal issues. The crimes that involve one account, one suspect, one victim, or one event are going to be tricky because the cloud service may not be willing to help you out. As always, it depends on which side of the conflict you're on.

Issues with Cloud Forensics

1. No jurisdiction over data. Most cloud providers have redundant data centers located in several places throughout the world.

2. Massive increase of cellular devices accessing/loading/creating/altering and moving data in the cloud. This means that data could be in several places at the same time.

3. No central role for management to help filter out suspects. You do not own the data storage, you are just renting it.

4. No access control to keep data segregated for a forensic investigation. Customers can get to that data at any moment, at any time.

5. Lack of physical infrastructure to create a time-line or determine timestamps or log events.

6. Terms and conditions between organization and Cloud provider may not allow a forensic investigation that will meet your requirements.

7. Retrieval of evidence without modifying it is extremely difficult.

8. Each cloud service handles their data storage and service conditions differently.

If a crime was committed against the cloud provider, the provider has the jurisdiction over that criminal activity. The cloud customer may have limited or no access to cloud data, more so, if the social media site owns that data. This is the case with services such as Facebook, where the content is user driven but owned by the cloud service. (Are you surprised to find that your user content is owned by the social media site, not you?)

Exercises

8.36   There are a few techniques that work if you are trying to identify the sender of data unless that sender uses a proxy. Chrome and certain add-ons to FireFox allow you to view the content of HTTP source. How can you use the information this reveals to block the sender? Do so on your browser.

Conclusion for Counter Forensics

Digital forensics is not an easy task, nor it is an easy profession. You must be detail oriented, able to document everything you do to the evidence you find, think like a criminal and have an enormous amount of patience to locate all the evidence. Besides that, you need to be willing and able to be an expert witness, if called to testify in a case.

On the other hand, some education and experience with forensics techniques and tools can help you maintain the privacy and confidentiality you've been losing fast in our digital world.

If you were brave enough to complete this lesson, you know we discussed where media comes into play as source to hide data, boot up a computer and hide evidence within data or within the operating system. You were introduced to some very tricky places that data can be hidden and how to thwart forensic experts.

Digital forensics is filled with areas that require expert knowledge or at least a fairly good understanding of that area. This lesson was designed to provide you a taste of what you can expect if you want to work in this amazing field – or just be an informed computer user.

Alphabetical Index

NO WORRIES!
OSSTMMTRAINING.ORG

KNOWING HOW TO APPLY THE OSSTMM TAKES YOUR WORRIES AWAY.
OSSTMM TRAINING MAKES YOU A BETTER, MORE EFFICIENT SECURITY TESTER
AND ANALYST WHICH MAKES WHAT YOU NEED TO SECURE BE MORE SECURE.

ISECOM

Made in the USA
Las Vegas, NV
25 November 2024